The Lake Superior Agate
One Man's Journey

by Scott F. Wolter

outernet
publishing, LLC

President   Jon K. Earl
Publisher   Don Beimborn
Copy Editor   Nancy Sauro
Cover and Text Designer   Jennifer Wreisner

ISBN 1-58175-207-5

Published by Outernet Publishing, LLC
9995 West 69th Street
Eden Prairie, MN 55344
(800)848-2707
www. outernetpublishing.com

Printed in the United States of America
10 9 8 7 6 5 4 3 2 1

Dedication

To my two beautiful babies, Grant and Amanda, who give me hope and inspiration everyday.

Cover Painting

"One-In-A-Million"

An agate collecting families' fantasy. The moment before the many hours of searching for the rare "big one", is rewarded. What better place to have it happen than along a secluded beach on the North Shore of Lake Superior.

When I first told Dan Wiemer about the idea of doing a painting for the cover of my new book, he was as excited as I was. Dan has a combination of attributes that made him perfect for this project. He's a highly talented artist, a very nice guy and an avid Lake Superior agate collector. Dan has captured my vision of this fantasy agate collecting scene, perfectly.

You can contact Dan at: Dan Wiemer Illustrations
                            545 Spring Creek Ave. S.
                            Red Wing, Minn. 55066
                            651-388-8047 Fax 651-267-0360

You can contact Scott at: Lake Superior Agate, Inc.
                            P.O. Box 14611
                            Minneapolis, Minn. 55414
                            952-934-6597
                            www.lakesuperioragate.com

Table of Contents

Introduction

I am an addict. There, I said it. They say the first part of dealing with an addiction is being able to admit it. Now that I've done that, I'm sure it would help to share my story of how I became hooked on Lake Superior agates. When did I realize that I had become an agate fanatic afflicted with what I like to call "agatitis"? It was shortly after I learned what a Lake Superior agate was. My college professor Charlie Matsch educated me about a rock I'd found while on a field trip along the North Shore. I was so fascinated by that little banded stone that I did everything I could to learn more about it. I researched whatever sparse literature I could find, and visited with people who were knowledgeable about agates. As I learned more about these pretty rocks, my appetite to find and collect them steadily increased.

Looking back now, I realize it was then that the agate bug bit me. What is it like to have this lifelong agate disease? After twenty years of being intimately involved with Lake Superior agates, I think I'm beginning to understand. In the beginning, I thought that collecting agates would follow the normal course of many of my passing interests. I'd start off hot and then slowly cool off until the next thing came along. For some reason, my strong initial interest in agates didn't fade; it just got stronger.

My passion for agates shows no sign of stopping. The overall interest in Lake Superior agates has grown, with a steadily increasing number of people enjoying the hobby. Along with the surge in interest has come an increase in the number of collectors and their incredible finds. This book shares my experiences with these wonderful rocks and tells how I put together a really nice collection. The beginning of a new millennium seems like a good time to stop and reflect on all that has happened so far. It is also an opportunity to do what I enjoy most about collecting Lake Superior agates, sharing these fantastic treasures with others who appreciate them.

I have reflected not only on my own affliction, but also on the many people I've met along the way whose agate "fever" has impacted on my life. In extreme cases like mine, the driving passion to pursue the beautiful banded state gemstone of Minnesota can only be called one thing-the fire.

My competitive "fire" for agates can sometimes be so strong that I've even resorted to begging. My efforts with Gary Ottman in 1994 however, were unsuccessful...but I'll keep trying!

The Fire

For twenty years now I've known about the burning drive in people to collect agates. But it wasn't until I was almost forty years old that a friend very clearly explained what having "the fire" meant. He was a teammate who knew that having a strong, passionate will was necessary for survival. In this case he wasn't talking about agates, he was talking about football.

In the summer of 1997, a friend named Todd Fultz approached me and asked if I would be interested in playing minor league football. He had been hired to coach a team called the Minneapolis Lumberjacks and was looking for players. Todd and I had played touch football together for several years. He was now talking to those of us he thought could still play tackle football. At first I said, "Yeah, right." My initial objection was only a lead-in for Todd to lay out his usually effective sales pitch. He went right for the juggler vein, my ego.

I was definitely intrigued, but this wasn't touch football he was talking about. This was full contact with helmets and shoulder pads. As Todd laid out the details, my mind wandered back in time with rationalization. I was a pretty fair linebacker in my college days at the University of Minnesota, Duluth. We won two conference championships and went undefeated my senior year. It would be fun to relive that glorious time. Just thinking about those days was a rush. I've certainly kept active over the years playing more than my share of sports, but that's not like playing real football, the greatest sport there is. The only problem was, that was seventeen years ago.

At thirty-eight years old, I should have thanked Todd for asking me and politely said no. Instead, the lure to relive the old glory was too great. I told him there was no way I should be doing this, but in the end I said, "I'm in!" When I got home and told Janet and the kids, they thought I was kidding. After explaining what Todd had presented, they realized that I meant it. Of course, the first thing Janet thought of was that I was going to get killed. Even as she tried to talk some sense into me, she knew it was no use. Janet looked at me and sighed. Putting some humor in the situation, she said, "I guess playing football isn't that bad of a midlife crisis. It's better than having an affair or buying a fancy sports car." My plan was to play one year, hopefully survive, and get out in one piece. After four seasons of some of the most fun I ever had, I retired in October 2000, two months short of my forty-second birthday. We won a championship ring, and best of all, I came out with all my limbs still functioning. It turned out to be a wonderful experience, not only for me, but for my family as well. Janet and my daughter, Amanda, cheered from the stands at nearly every game. One of the biggest thrills was having my son, Grant, on the sidelines with me as the team water boy. He did a great job, especially on one blistering August day when we played in 100-degree heat. I thought for sure I was going to die.

One of my favorite teammates was a guy named James Tucker. My partner in the middle was a 5' 10", 235-pound cannonball-like linebacker who hit like a ton. Tuck didn't talk much, but when he did, people listened. In all the years I played and watched football, I never saw a linebacker fly through and fill a hole like him. He would hit guys with everything he had, and usually that was all that was necessary. I loved playing with Tuck. He'd make a mess of running backs, and I'd come in and clean up the scraps. Many times

James Tucker (right) and myself walking out for the coin toss of the 1997 Mid-America Football League championship game at the Metrodome in Minneapolis, Minnesota.

I'd hear him laughing before and after he hit somebody. I used to think he was nuts. But after a while, I came to realize that what made him a good football player was a burning desire and love for the game.

At the start of my second season, a few of us were talking about a player who had just quit the team. The guy was a good, experienced player who'd practiced with us the first few days. We were speculating on why he quit when Tucker interrupted and said, "I know why he quit. He ain't got the fire, he ain't got the fire. When you ain't got the fire no more, it's all over and time to get the hell out!" We all looked at him and knew exactly what he meant. The fire is that passion and desire that gets in the way of logical thinking. It's what unleashes the adrenaline, pushes aside the pain, and keeps you running, hitting, and trying to win, no matter what. The fire is a powerful thing in football, but when it's gone, you're done.

The fire had not burned out in me when I decided to hang up the pads. I know how fortunate I was to have been able to enjoy that experience. Most of all, I feel lucky that I lived to tell about it. At forty-two years old, it was time to turn my energy and my fire to other things. You can probably guess what the other thing was.

The Early Agate Days

The first place I looked for agates, after finding that first one, was in decorative rock. I lived in an older house in Duluth during my college days, and I often walked to the Kentucky Fried Chicken on Superior Street for meals. As I walked up to the door, I saw the multicolored glacial rocks around the restaurant. I hardly noticed the people shaking their heads while watching me as I scanned the pea-sized gravel for little gemstones. My persistence was rewarded, and the hunt was on. From there I stopped at every place I could to look for agates in decorative rock. I walked around apartment buildings, businesses, parking lots, even around bridges and freeway medians looking for agates. I know I got the same puzzled look from people whizzing by in their cars wondering what that idiot along the road was looking for.

One memorable day, I made an important discovery on the way to visit my cousin in St. Paul. Patty lived in a high-rise apartment building, and as I walked up I saw it. The building was lined with glacial decorative rock, only these rocks were up to the size of a football! My normal enthusiasm was suddenly tempered because I didn't know if agates could get that big. I did know, however, that there was only one way to find out. I spent the next two hours scanning the rocks. When I was done I'd found four big agates, including a quartz ball that weighed about three pounds. Patty just laughed when I showed her my reasons for being late. The important discovery was that these awesome stones could get pretty big!

In those days, I rode a Kawasaki KZ-650 motorcycle, the perfect agate exploration vehicle. The bike was big enough to travel long distances on the highway, yet nimble enough to take off-road to sneak into the pits. I did that often. I used to bolt after classes and ride the twenty or so miles to pick agates in a gravel pit near Carlton. This particular pit was huge, and the owners didn't mind agate pickers coming in. The dark-gray, boulder-sized gravel was thick and rich in agate. I found many nice specimens and started a modest collection. I would neatly arrange my treasures on a bookshelf into perfectly straight rows according to size, small ones up front, big ones in the back. In the middle of the back row I had a pedestal made of Popsicle sticks for the "Agate of the Week." My roommates would look in on me, shaking their heads, probably thinking, "Geology major, good thing I picked marketing."

By the time I graduated in the spring of 1982, my little collection was pretty impressive, I thought. The largest quality agate I had was about twelve ounces. I found my first good big one in the summer of 1983. I had started my first job in geology working for a mineral exploration company, looking for gold in northern Minnesota. I was living with four others in a small hotel in Cook, Minnesota. We affectionately called ourselves "swamp rats," which was a well deserved title. Six days a week we trudged through seemingly endless bogs and swamps with heavily loaded backpacks. We carried thirty feet of connecting aluminum pipes that we hand-drilled into the floating bogs, collecting basal peat samples. The peat and clay at the bottom of the bogs contained minerals, including gold, that had weathered from the rock at the bottom. We would also peel back the moss from exposed bedrock to map and collect samples. It was the hardest and most physically challenging job I've ever had. At the end of each day, my legs ached from hauling the up to fifty-pound pack. My feet were always wet and wrinkly from being soaked in cold, mucky water. Everyday my swamp boots filled with water from stepping into a hole in the bog. I still have nightmares about being attacked by swarms of mosquitoes, which no doubt are flashbacks from those days in the swamps.

On one of my most memorable outings, I nearly had to spend a night alone in the swamp. My boss, Ernie Downs, pulled out the topographic maps at breakfast and said, "Scott, you've got a long hike today." We studied the map and decided that to get the best samples and get out before dark, I'd have to traverse almost eight miles. The worst part was that I had to cross two creeks in the swamps. Oh, those creeks were terrible! Whenever you approached them, you had to step on clumps of floating bog brush that slowly sank under your weight. Most of the time you'd fall over and get soaked. By the time you reached the creek itself, it was never a width that you could step or jump across. I usually had to swim across with that wet pack full of pipe and peat samples.

My four "swamp rat" comrades in the field near Cook, Minnesota. Second from left was our fearless leader Ernie Downs.

To top it off, these were cedar swamps with twisted trees and roots sticking out that seemed to purposely try to trip you and break your ankle.

As I finished my breakfast and studied the map, I noticed that I'd be walking over areas with iron formation, where my compass would be useless. I looked up at Ernie, with that ever-present smile and upbeat attitude, and he said, "It will be a challenge, but you can do it." If it wasn't for the fact that he had made many tough treks like this himself, I probably would have been upset. The plan was for me to hit the old Taconite Trail at the end of the day and walk the final mile to the road where Ernie would pick me up. After Ernie's pep talk, I was ready to go. We drove to the drop-off point, and I entered the woods as the early morning sky began to lighten. It was an overcast day with very low cloud cover and an intermittent drizzle. I thought, "It figures."

The trek was as tough as promised, but with each step you tell yourself you're that much closer to a hot shower and a good meal. By dinnertime I was running late. I was knee-deep in a swamp, with cedar trees doing their best to slow me down. My pack was soaked and full of samples, and it must have weighed close to sixty pounds. I pressed onward, trying to find the trail, but it wasn't where it was supposed to be. Since I couldn't use the sun to get my bearings, I was relying solely on my compass. As I walked in what I was sure was a straight line, the arrow on my compass kept moving to the right. Suddenly it hit me-I was walking over an iron formation. My compass was useless. I remember the cold chill that ran down my spine when I realized I might be in that awful swamp all night long. I stopped and peered through the trees. I thought I saw a slight clearing and walked over to check it. I stepped up a foot or so onto hard ground and realized it was an old railroad bed. It was the Taconite Trail and my ticket out of there. It turned out that I had been walking parallel to it. If I had followed my compass heading, I would have walked right back in the direction I had come from. Whew! Now all I had to do was walk out.

It was just beginning to get dark as I looked down the long, straight trail that was overgrown with trees and brush. As I started out, it felt like I was walking through a tunnel. The wind was blowing through the treetops, but it was calm on the trail as I walked and fantasized about the burgers and beer I would have for dinner. I still had almost a mile to go when I looked up and suddenly froze in my tracks. About a hundred yards ahead of me a huge timber wolf had emerged from the swamp and was trotting toward me. His head was down, and I was sure he hadn't seen me-yet. The wind was blowing across the trail so he hadn't smelled me either. I slowly reached over my shoulder and grabbed a five-foot section of drill pipe. It was fight or flee, and I sure wasn't going back into that swamp. He got within about fifty yards when he suddenly stopped. He picked his head up and sniffed the air. He must have caught a whiff of my ripe odor, and he quickly dashed into the swamp. My sigh of relief was cut short when I realized I still had to walk by where he had disappeared. It was pitch black when I finally hit the road, but good old Ernie was waiting for me. He could tell by the look on my face that it had been a tough day.

The job was mentally challenging, as well, since there weren't many people to socialize with in Cook. We spent most of our free time alone in our rooms. Other than the long phone calls from my girlfriend, Janet, I had only one other fun thing to look forward to-Sunday, my day off. Since Cook was north of the glacial agate boundary, I was on my bike before sunup, speeding south to the gravel pits to find treasure and my sanity. On one trip I found a relatively small pit along Highway 2 west of Duluth that looked pretty good for finding agates. It had rained hard the night before, and there were washouts and puddles all over. I'd only found a couple chips of agate and was getting ready to move on when I spotted it. A solid gray and white agate with a red center was lying in a washout. It looked huge! I quickly washed it off in a puddle and stashed it into the windjammer on my bike. That night back at my motel room, I cleaned my newest prize before placing it with pride atop the Agate of the Week Popsicle-stick pedestal.

My modest agate collection in February 1984. The three-pound giant from the J & M Rock Shop is on the far left. The 1.38-pound gray-and-white I found near Duluth is sitting on the "agate of the week" popsicle-stick stand in the middle of the back row.

The Trip to
Australia

By the end of October, after three and a half months, the swamp-rat gold project was over. Ernie said I had done a good job and offered me a full-time position. The next project was to start in January, again looking for gold. This time the field-work would be in the mountains of Nevada. He said, "If you can make it through a project like this, you can make it through anything." I knew that nothing could be this tough and things would only get better. I accepted the job and excitedly rode back home to the Twin Cities for a two-month break.

I moved back in with my parents to rest up and prepare to head out into the world. This time it would be for good. After a couple of days, my dad and I talked about me taking a vacation before I started the next project. My father, Fred Addison Wolter, had been a pilot with Northwest Airlines for twenty-five years. One of the great benefits our family enjoyed were generous travel privileges. My brother, Greg, and sister, Danna, and I often took advantage of the opportunity while growing up. Since I was done with school, and no longer considered a dependent, my days of flying on passes were just about over.

Dad said, "You have one pass left. Whatever trip you want to take, make it a good one." A trip to a warm climate with clean, clear water sounded really good. I had been a certified scuba diver since I was sixteen and, I actively pursued the hobby. My father and Greg were also divers. I had already been to many wonderful places to scuba dive, but I had never been to Australia's Great Barrier Reef. When I told him where I wanted to go, he said, "Great, who do you want to go with?" Since my father, Greg, and one of my best friends were all divers, I could have taken the trip with any one of them. After thinking a few moments, I decided that I wanted to take the trip of a lifetime with him. Dad was surprised and excited. I knew right away that I had made the right choice and that we would have a great time.

Over the next month we laid out our plans and worked out to get in shape. We were going to be traveling for four weeks, and we wanted to be both mentally and physically prepared. At fifty-two, Dad was still in great physical shape. As the days went by leading up to our departure, the way I normally pictured my father changed. Instead of having to work around the head of the household to get my way, I began to realize what a great guy he was. I always loved my father, but like most people, the teenage years were often a challenge. While in college, I was fortunate enough to figure out how good I had it growing up, and he was the biggest reason. Not only would he be a lot of fun on the trip, but his experience gained from many years of flying to the Orient would no doubt come in handy.

On November 26, 1983, with our tent, sleeping bags, clothes, and scuba gear packed, we took off for our first stop in Los Angeles, California. We spent the next three days bodysurfing and hiking on the island of Oahu in Hawaii. On the third night of camping on the beach, a flashlight poked inside our tent and woke us up. A police officer, in the process of kicking us off the beach, asked Dad for his identification. I remember the officer's puzzled look when he realized this "bum" was a Northwest Airlines captain. Dad explained that this was his son's trip and that camping out was my idea. No doubt an oceanfront hotel with a soft bed would have been his preference. The officer shrugged and said, "Make sure you're out of here in the morning." The smooth way Dad handled the officer told me he'd been in delicate situations before. That episode on the beach reminded me of an especially delicate situation that Dad handled beautifully.

My dad catches a nice wave on Sandy Beach during our three days in Oahu, Hawaii.

In January 1971, I was twelve years old and walking home from school one day with my brother and sister. Dad was away on a trip and my mother Barbara was home alone. As we walked up the driveway, she burst out the front door and said, "Your father's been hijacked!" Danna and Greg were confused, but I knew by the fear in Mom's face that this was not good. A twenty-year-old man boarded Dad's flight in Milwaukee, Wisconsin, and on the way to Washington, D.C., he entered the cockpit. He asked for the captain and dad spoke up. The man put a hatchet to Dad's head and said he had a bomb in his briefcase. He said he wanted to go to Algiers in Africa or he would blow up the plane. My father kept his cool and told him they didn't have enough fuel to fly over the Atlantic. He suggested Cuba instead. Dad told us later that they did have the fuel to make it, but he was worried that if they went to Algiers they might not come back. The frightened man agreed, and they landed in Havana a few hours later. The passengers and crew were detained for four days and then returned safely back to the United States. The hijacker was jailed, and as it turned out, he did have a bomb in the briefcase. He spent ten awful years in Cuban custody before being returned to the United States to be prosecuted.

When everyone returned to Minneapolis, they were greeted like heroes and Dad was the star of the show. The entire crew came through in the clutch, but my dad was the one in charge. Whenever people look back on their life and think about their one shining moment in the sun, this was definitely his day. We were all proud of him then, and we're proud of him now.

Our next stop was Tokyo, Japan. Dad had been there many times and knew exactly where to go and what to do. At one point we took a subway train to a busy marketplace to do some shopping. I'll never forget how crowded that city was. When we first got onto the train we were standing right next to each other. By the time the rush of people had stopped, I looked back and there were twenty people

My dad and I clown around at the Minneapolis/St. Paul airport press conference in January 1971. All passengers and crew returned safely from Cuba after their flight from Milwaukee, Wisconsin, to Washington, D.C., was hijacked.

OFFICE OF
GENERAL MANAGER
FLIGHT OPERATIONS

NORTHWEST AIRLINES, INC.

MINNEAPOLIS–ST. PAUL INTERNATIONAL AIRPORT

ST. PAUL, MINNESOTA 55111

March 4, 1971

Dear Captain Wolter:

On behalf of Northwest Airlines, Inc., please accept our congratulations in the professional manner in which you carried out your hi-jacked flight 334 on January 22, 1971.

Both you and ourselves can look back with pride at the job you performed under the difficulty of the situation.

Enclosed are copies of most all of the reports of the flight which you might wish to keep in your memoirs. You have joined a somewhat "elite" group.

We are proud of the job you and your crew accomplished. Again, my congratulations and many thanks.

Sincerely yours,

W. F. Hochbrunn, Jr.

W. F. Hochbrunn, Jr.

Encls.

CC: Employee Records
    LPLowinske

Captain Fred Wolter
Minneapolis, Minnesota

The letter of commendation to Dad from Northwest Airlines.

between us. We were packed so tight I couldn't lift my arms up to hold the handrail. As it turned out, I didn't need to; I couldn't have fallen over if I had wanted to.

While browsing through a department store, I found bags of rocks for sale. When I looked closer, I realized they were tumble-polished agates from China. They were yellow-brown in color and reminded me a little of lakers. I couldn't resist and bought a bag. I still have the biggest one, about a half-pounder.

From there we spent a day in Hong Kong, and then it was off to the "land down under." We spent the seventh day traveling from the capital city of Sydney to the northeastern coast city of Cairns. While the plane was descending, we looked out the window and could see the vast and beautiful Great Barrier Reef. We were close to our final destination. I suddenly got that shiver of excitement from the anticipation of taking the first dive. Tomorrow would be our first venture into the crown jewel of scuba diving.

We pitched our tent in a campground outside of town and had a couple of beers by the campfire. We talked about how lucky we were, earlier in the day, to have found a boat captain kind enough to take us out on the reef the next morning. Dad wasn't much of a drinker and quickly fell asleep. I remember watching him as he slept and thinking how cool all this was. For the rest of my life I'll be happy that I thanked him that night for this trip and all the good things I had growing up. I don't know if it was a premonition, or maturity, that initiated my reflection. Either way, my timing turned out to be perfect.

We woke the next morning to a warm and humid tropical day. The sun was up and the temperature would reach 103 degrees that day. We showed up at the dock and there was quite a crowd gathered at the boat. There were about thirty people with twenty-five or so of them skin divers who were participating in a spearfishing contest. The three-hour trip out to the reef went quickly, and we had a great time. It turned out that this

My dad and I flash a smile while scuba diving in an underwater cave off Grand Cayman Island in 1980.

group went out regularly, and everyone was very friendly to the two Yanks who had crashed their party. Dad and I invited a bunch of them to play a card game called "elimination." There was a huge table bolted to the deck in the cabin, and at least a dozen people crowded around to play. We needed about four decks of cards. It's a simple game. Everybody gets seven cards to start with, and you have to take at least one trick to get into the next round. High card takes the trick unless it gets trumped. The person with the most tricks gets to call trump the next round after looking at the cards in hand. Each round one less card is dealt to each player. If you don't take a trick, you're eliminated. The last person in wins.

We played several games and roared with laughter as people were eliminated when they thought they were safe. The last game came down to two players and two cards. My dad called trump, and being a good card player, it seemed a lock that he would win. The other player, one of two brothers we had met, never did understand what he was doing in the game. The funny part was everyone else knew it, too. Everyone on the boat was crowded around the table to watch the final hand. Dad sat there confidently as his opponent stared at his cards without a clue as to what to do. He slowly played his cards and, amazingly, took both tricks to win the game. Everybody erupted in laughter at the obvious irony, and nobody laughed harder than my dad.

Shortly before we reached the reef, I remember thinking that this was the highlight of the trip so far. It was a perfect day, we were meeting fun and interesting people, and we were about to accomplish the main goal of the trip. It doesn't get any better than this, I thought. A few minutes after the card game, the captain anchored in a shallow tidal channel. The reef was about eight to ten feet deep with a channel about forty yards wide and fifteen to twenty feet deep. Dad and I talked about this being the perfect situation; it was a shallow and easy first dive. The twenty-five or so competitors put on their masks, fins, and snorkels, jumped into the water, and hurried off to the reef. Since Dad and I were guests, we waited until everyone else was gone before putting on our scuba gear and jumping in. As soon as we surfaced, we could feel the strong current. The tide was moving out to sea with the bulk of the water flowing through the channels. It felt like we were diving in a swiftly flowing river. The sea was choppy, with waves tossing us around a little bit.

After briefly collecting ourselves, Dad looked over at me and gave the OK sign. He then pointed up-current for me to take the lead. We had previously agreed to swim into the current at the start, leaving an easier swim back. I started to descend and began adjusting my buoyancy by blowing into my buoyancy compensator (BC). My attention to my partner had been distracted for only a few seconds when I realized Dad was no longer with me. I quickly surfaced to locate him, but he wasn't there. I swam around the boat, surfacing repeatedly, but I couldn't find him. I remember being a little annoyed that he would swim off without me. I eventually went far enough that I could see where we had jumped into the water, from the other side of the boat. No sign of him. At that moment, I thought he must be way up in front of the boat, and swam up current to find him. Little did I know, he was in serious trouble, being carried by the current in the other direction.

After about twenty minutes of searching, I was beginning to get upset with him. I decided to swim back to the boat. When I started up the ladder, I was met by the brother who had won the card game. I began to ask if he had seen my father, when I noticed a look of dread on his face. Before I could say another word, I saw my dad's body on the deck. The skin divers had already pulled him out. I couldn't believe it. I felt as though I had been hit in the head with a brick. My whole body was numb. When I looked into his eyes, I knew that he was gone. Somehow, right under my nose, my dad had drowned.

How could this happen? It was a hot, beautiful day. I was enjoying my favorite hobby, at the greatest place in the world to do it. On top of everything, I was doing it with my dad. The whole time we were in the water and while I was searching for him, I never had an inkling that anything was wrong. It was that lack of a sense of urgency that would haunt me constantly for two years. My life changed forever that day.

For the next two days I was in a dream like state, waiting for the nightmare to end. The three-hour boat ride back seemed like an eternity. I didn't leave his side for a moment. The two brothers on the boat, who lived in Cairns, took me into their home and looked out for me. I don't know why they bothered to get involved, but I'm very grateful they did. They were so kind to me. A coroner did an autopsy and found no evidence of a medical condition or any kind of animal attack. The death certificate said salt-water drowning. What the hell happened! I still can't figure it out. My father was well-trained for emergencies and had a cool demeanor-it just didn't make sense.

The police held an inquest to try to determine what had happened. One of the skin divers testified that he was tired and on his way back to the boat when he saw him near the bottom. With tears in his eyes, he told about swimming down to try to help him. He said he grabbed him by his buoyancy compensator to try and pull him up, but ran out of breath. He said he almost drowned himself, and had to get back to the boat. I felt terrible for him because he had a chance to save him, but couldn't. He also said when he first looked down, Dad was trying to take his air tank off. When I heard this, I knew that he had panicked and was fighting for his life. The anguish was suffocating as I listened to his story. I couldn't understand it; all Dad had to do was pull on either one of two emergency CO2 cartridges. They would have instantly filled his BC with air and brought him to the surface. I had given him that BC before we left as an early Christmas present, thinking it would be safer. The whole thing created more questions for me than answers. The most agonizing thing was that while all this was going on, I was off looking for him in the wrong place. I had no clue what was happening. No matter what anybody ever says, I was not there to help him and I should have been.

After two of the longest days of my life, all I wanted to do was go home, although it almost killed me when I had to leave him there. His body wouldn't come back for almost two more weeks. On the plane ride home, my mother's words kept echoing in my head, "Make sure you take good care of your father." The days and weeks that followed could not have been worse. Everyone in our family was devastated, and I felt like it was my fault. For a while, I wasn't sure if I was going to make it. I tried to handle my grief as best I could and kept in mind a phrase I like to say when something bad happens: "When one door closes, another one opens up somewhere." I didn't know it at the time, but another door had opened.

What does this tragic event have to do with agates? Everything! I know I'm not the first person to go through an awful life experience. I've met many people since that day who have had tragedy in their lives. What I have come to realize is that it is what you do after tragedy that is important. For nearly two years, I really struggled. I declined the job in Nevada and decided to stay home. The job market for geologists in Minnesota at that time was meager, to say the least. I ended up working odd sales jobs that I hated. If it wasn't for Janet, I don't know if I would have made it. She was there for me the whole time, and believe me, I was no fun to be around. I also had my hobby. The agates helped me more than I could ever have dreamed. The grief and guilt were often overwhelming. The only way I could calm myself was to head for the gravel pits. I'd walk for hours looking for agates-and answers. At least I had success finding agates. Anyone who picks agates knows that a little success can lead to compulsion. I quickly became consumed with picking because it always made me feel better.

My addiction quickly evolved to the point where I wasn't satisfied with the agates that I could find in the field. I had certainly found some nice specimens, but hardly any of meaningful size. I quickly learned that there were nice agates to be had that were a pound and more in size, but they were found in people's basements, not the gravel pit. On a trip to Duluth in the spring of 1984, I made a fateful decision in the J & M Rock Shop. I paid money for an agate. Talk about opening Pandora's box! The small shop had Lake Superior agates of all sizes for sale. Up until this moment, I had only the rocks I found on my own. After looking at some of the beautiful big ones in this shop and thinking about how hard it was to find them, I started to rethink my position. I soon found myself pondering a three-pound giant that was the prettiest agate I had ever seen. I told myself I had to have it. The only trouble was the $150 price. Somehow I came up with the money, and the prize was mine. Soon after however, like any other addict, I needed another fix.

"One of My Better Throws"

Besides frequenting rock shops, I began to network with other collectors to see what big agates were out there. Almost every weekend I'd jump on my bike or get in the car to seek out other rock hounds. Those early quests to find agate collectors and their treasures produced many memorable adventures. One of the more humorous and, as it turned out, fateful trips, came after a visit with the family of a close friend. My college roommate, Bruce Grant, invited me to have dinner at his parents' home one night. After the meal, Bruce and his father Bud and I sat down to visit. We talked about sports, family, and the trip to Australia. Eventually, the conversation turned to agates when Bruce interjected, "Dad, whatever happened to that big agate you had as a kid?" My ears immediately perked up, and I looked over at his dad. Bud gave him a puzzled look as Bruce gestured with his hands. He made a ball that was about the size of a softball and said, "You remember, the one about this size."

Bud is the legendary Minnesota Vikings football coach whom I'd admired for years. He has a spotless reputation, and his word was gold to me. What I was to eventually learn was that he had a legendary sense of humor, also. Before he uttered a word, I had already swallowed the bait.

My buddy Bruce Grant and I celebrate winning a touch football tournament in the fall of 1989.

"What agate? How big was it? Where is it now?" Bud looked at me deadpan as could be and said, "I threw it into the lake!". Incredulous, I blurted out, "What lake? Where is it? How far did you throw it?" He paused and said, "Up at the cabin, and you know, it was one of my better throws."

At first I was stunned with disbelief. How could he do such a thing to a big agate? Even though I was filled with horror over the agate, my mind started working. Bud grew up in Superior, Wisconsin which is prime Lake Superior agate country. An avid hunter and fisherman, he has spent a lot of time outdoors. He certainly could have found a big agate along the way. I thought, "He probably didn't understand how rare the agate he found was." I began to devise a plan.

I knew their cabin was in a northern Wisconsin area that probably had sandy-bottom lakes. Bud was a great athlete and former professional baseball player, so I was sure he could have launched the rock a long way. However, with my scuba gear, I was sure I could find it. I quickly laid out my plan to them, not pausing for a moment to thoroughly check out their story. I asked if it would be all right to go up and try to find it. They both chuckled, not believing I'd really pursue the idea, then Bud said, "Sure, have at it." The agate bug had bitten once again, hard this time!

My college roommate Mark Brugman finds a gem during the stampede at the 1989 Moose Lake Agate Days.

Mark Brugman snapped this picture just before I swam off to find the phantom agate Bud Grant threw into the lake.

It had been almost six months since the trip to Australia, and this seemed like the perfect opportunity to go back into the water. It took a couple of weeks, but I talked another college roommate, Mark Brugman, to come with me on the trip. We loaded my scuba gear into the car and headed north into Wisconsin on a Friday night. Mark was also into agates, although not nearly as fanatical. We fantasized about the big agate and whether or not I'd find it. If the lake bottom was sandy, there shouldn't be too many other big rocks, so I felt pretty confident. Two and a half hours later, we arrived at the cabin and both fell asleep in the car.

We awoke at day break and quickly unloaded the car. The shore was sandy in both directions, and my hopes quickly soared. Mark helped me into my wet suit and with the air tank. Once I was ready, I backed slowly into the water as Mark took a spotter position on the dock. I checked my equipment and air flow, then gave Mark the thumbs-up sign. As I slowly made my descent, I scanned the sandy bottom. The water was very clear, and after only a few feet, I found my first soft-ball-sized rock. It was covered with a little bit of sediment, but when I picked it up and shook it, I could easily make out the rock type. Everything was perfect. If that agate was there, I'd find it for sure.

I decided to swim in a criss-crossing pattern straight out from the dock. I saw numerous fish, rocks, and an occasional tree branch or log, and I made sure to search the bottom to the maximum distance from the dock that I thought Bud could throw. I had been in the fifteen-foot deep water for twenty minutes when the cold cloud of reality suddenly set in. I'd been duped. There was no agate. At first I was mad, but as I swam back to shore I started to realize it was my own fault. Both Bruce and his dad felt bad that the joke went further than they ever intended. Even after I asked if I could go up to their cabin, they didn't really think I would do it. When I surfaced and walked out of the water, I looked up at Mark. He was shaking his head at me. Another victim of the agate bug.

After the phantom agate fiasco, Mark and I jumped in the car and continued north to Superior, Wisconsin, to follow up another big agate lead. We met fellow agate collector John Moin at the Lignell Drugstore who steered us to Duluth and the fateful meeting with George Flaim. A weekend trip that started off a little "rocky" ended up being the most important weekend in my agate-collecting life.

George Flaim

The first big agate I bought from George was the 2.12 pounder I call the Royal Flaim. Of all the wonderful agates in George's basement, it was the one that caught my eye first. When he said he wanted $400 for it, my heart sank. Not because the agate wasn't worth it, but because I couldn't afford it. The three-pound monster I had paid $150 for a couple weeks earlier had pretty much broken the bank. When I explained this to him, he said, "Give me what you can now and take it, you can pay me the rest later!" I was shocked by how trusting he was and decided to take

him up on his offer. I gave him a $150 down payment and then rode happily home to Minneapolis with my new treasure. After a week or so, guilt replaced my joy when the realization that the balance owed on the agate was nowhere in sight. At the end of the second week, I put the agate in a box and sent it back to George. I wrote a note saying that I'd be back for it when I could afford it. I don't remember how I did it, but in less than a month I was knocking on George's door, with all the money this time.

From that point on our agate dealings quickly escalated. George was the dealer and I was the addict. It's amazing how motivated one can be when you really want

George Flaim's awesome collection is strewn on his basement floor during that first visit in March 1984.

something. Over the next several months, I made numerous trips to Duluth to see George and his wife, Elaine. I often brought Janet or a buddy along to meet my new friend and to see his amazing agates. George and Elaine were always gracious, and I never left the house without something new.

On one of those early visits, I was trying to figure out if there might be something else I could bargain with besides money. Since I was far from being well-heeled, I figured there must be other things that George might trade agates for. When I asked him he said, "Sure, I love Parker shotguns and white-tailed deer antlers." We got up and went into the back room of his basement, where he showed me a few of his deer heads. Even though I wasn't a hunter, I could appreciate how impressive they were. The racks on these deer were incredible. My favorites were the non-typical racks. They had tines popping out all over the place. Some of those antlers looked like a bowl spaghetti. He also showed me a few of his impressive shotguns. Just like his agates, everything was top-notch.

As I listened to George tell me the history of each set of antlers, the wheels in my head started turning. There was a pretty nice set of antlers that I knew of, and they belonged to me. The minute I thought of them, my excitement about a possible trade began to ebb. First, I assumed the antlers I had couldn't be worth much to a big collector like George. The second reason was that this particular deer had a lot of sentimental value. I decided to tell him about them anyway.

In the fall of 1974, I was in tenth grade. We were living on a lake in Chanhassen, Minnesota, and my brother, Greg, and I used to love riding minibikes. We had these great little Honda CT-70s, and we would go tearing through the woods, along trails that wound around the lake. My dad also had a motorcycle and would often ride with us. On this particular day, Greg and I were on the other side of the lake riding through some thick cattails. I was oldest, so I went first. We were putzing along slowly, standing on our foot-pegs trying to see where we were going. Suddenly, this huge buck stood up in front of us. I instantly jumped off my bike, thinking he was going to charge us. Instead, he took a couple of steps and fell down. I wasn't sure what was going on, but we slowly turned around and went home to get our father. He jumped on his motorcycle, and we all rode back to where the deer was. He was still in the same spot. We concluded that he was injured and went back home and called the Department of Natural Resources (DNR). An officer came out that same day. The game officer said the deer had probably been hit by a car. He pointed out how thin the deer looked and how the vegetation around him had been eaten. He estimated that he may have been there a couple of weeks or more.

Eventually, he decided to end its misery and shot it. It was a shame, but it was the right thing to do. While the game officer was gutting the animal and preparing to drag it out, my dad came up with an idea. He wanted to make leather gloves out of the hide and offered to buy the carcass. The game officer said, "Give me $10 and it's yours." Dad gave him the money, and Greg and I ended up with the honor of dragging it out. It turned out that the hide was useless for tanning because gangrene had set in. We decided to have the head mounted instead. When Dad died, it ended up with me.

I told George the story, and he understood my sentiment. He said that I should still bring it up sometime so he could see it. The next trip up, I brought it along. When I showed it to George, I was surprised by his reaction. He pulled out a tape measure and scored the antlers. I had never heard of this before. George explained the Boone and Crockett scoring system and said my antlers, made the book. He said he liked them and was interested in a deal if I was. The agate collector in me was excited at being able to trade for an agate or two and not have to spend money that I didn't have. On the other hand, this head represented the memory of a special time I spent with my father and would be awfully hard to part with. While mulling it over, I went ahead and picked out two beautiful agates that were about two pounds each. It was decision time. George didn't pressure me at all. In the end, the pull of the agates was too strong. I went ahead and made the trade. As tough a decision as it was, I felt better thinking about the two new agates. I also knew that nothing could take away my memories.

As I thanked George for the agates and made my way to the door, he told me to stop by the house on Sunday before I headed back to the Twin Cities. It was Friday night, and I was planning on staying with friends on the North Shore for the weekend. A day and a half later, I walked into his basement, and George was standing there with the deer head in his hands. He said, "Here, I want you to have your dad's deer head back." I looked closer and realized the antlers were different. He had taken the original ones out and replaced them with another set. I asked if he wanted the agates back and he said, "No way, all I wanted were the antlers." I was in shock. I couldn't believe he could switch them that fast, let alone give the head back to me, for nothing in return. Forty years as a taxidermist had something to do with his skills, but his kindness was something he's always had. I drove home a happy boy that day!

A couple of years later, we did another agate trade, and I ended up getting the original antlers back. Once again, George did his magic and put them back on the original mount. Whenever people ask how I got the big deer head that hangs in our house, I smile and say, "If you have a couple of minutes, it's a great story."

As much as I loved seeing agates and doing deals on my visits, I enjoyed the time spent just visiting with George even more. We often talked for hours about things other than agates. He has led a full and fascinating life. I often sat riveted, listening to a master storyteller share his life experiences. The war stories fascinated me the most. George served four years in the military during World War II, including twenty-two months in the combat zone of the South Pacific. Born and raised as a baby boomer and never serving in the military, I will never know what it is like to put your life on the line defending your country. He told me how he survived being shot down in a B-25 bomber, and crashing on Mendenowa Island of the Phillippines in 1944. He suffered serious wounds to his shoulder and face. The last shrapnel fragments were removed from his face twenty-two years later.

George once had thirty-one starving Japanese soldiers surrender to him alone while he was on patrol. The soldiers had no choice, they had run out of food and their rifles had locked up and couldn't fire from the sweltering heat and humidity of the islands. We laughed at the irony when he told me that he was probably hungrier than they were. To top it off, the rifle he was carrying was also locked up. He still has the red and white Japanese flag they used to surrender with hanging on his basement wall. George is a true American hero. He is also the undisputed king of Lake Superior agate collecting. I have met people who had more agates than George, but nobody else is even close to when it comes to quality. George puts a high value on shape as well as size, color, and banding. That was one of the things that rubbed off on me. He also taught me a few tricks about what to do with agates that have a minor flaw or two. Unfortunately, I've been sworn to secrecy. Often, after taking a close look, I can see the tell-tale sign that an agate has been through George's hands, and it always makes me smile. For me, these agates take on a little extra value.

As an agate picker, I can't think of anyone else who has found more good big ones than he has. His colorful tales about his agate travels had a huge impact on my thirst for agates. He's made my whole agate experience richer and fuller. If Charlie Matsch was the one who infected me with agatitis, George is the one who made the disease explode. I look back now at those early visits and cherish the time we spent together at such an important time for me. George helped fill the void my fathers passing left, and I'll always be grateful to him for that. After almost seventeen years, I still see him as a father figure as well as a good friend.

Low altitude B-25 bombers during a run over a Japanese runway on a South Pacific island in 1944. The twenty-four-pound bombs called daisy-cutters, had parachutes to buy the planes enough time to get away before the explosions started. George said they destroyed seventeen planes that day. Military photographs were cut in half during the war for censorship and to prevent reprinting for profit.

The thirty-one Japanese soldiers being guarded by military police shortly after their surrender.

Recovering from malaria and dysentary, a twenty-two-year-old George Flaim proudly displays the Japanese flag given to him by the leader of the surrendering outfit. The signatures of the thirty-one soldiers who surrendered are on the flag.

Janet and George take a rest while picking agates near Moose Lake, Minnesota, in the summer of 1987.

The Lake Superior Agate

On one visit, sometime in the fall of 1985, he and I were talking about the lack of literature about Lake Superior agates. At one point, George looked at me and said, "Kid, you've got the geological knowledge, you've got the agate-picking experience, write the book!" Perhaps it was fate, but I didn't even think twice. My mind was made up right then and there. On the drive back to the Twin Cities, I wrote the outline for a book on the steering wheel as I drove. From that moment on I had a goal to focus on and never looked back.

Shortly before George's fateful words, I landed a great opportunity. One of the principals at Twin City Testing in St. Paul, Terry Swor, hired me as a field geologist. I finally got the break I needed to get back into the field of geology. It also was a decent-paying job, which besides helping to finance my agate addiction would help in paying for publishing the agate book.

The writing came easy, and with winter settling in, I had more time to do it. I started writing on my breaks at work since I had plenty of time in the office. When the fieldwork stopped, I was supposed to be reading testing procedures and technical papers. I couldn't wait for my daily breaks, so I could put down the boring stuff and write about agates. It didn't take long before "writing break" stretched from the allotted fifteen minutes, to an hour or more. It eventually got to the point where I felt so guilty about writing, I had to confess to my supervisor, Tom Flick. When I told him what I was doing, he said, "Oh, can I see it?" I gave him my chapters and essays and left his office feeling puzzled. A day later he called me back to his office and shocked me with what he said.

It turned out that Tom was a journalism major in college and was genuinely interested in what I was doing. He looked at me and said, "This is much more interesting than reading all that technical crap; Write your book!" I couldn't believe my ears. It would be the first of many good breaks I received while working on my project.

From then on I wrote and did research for the book every day over the winter months. Amazingly, I collected a paycheck every two weeks, too! Tom helped by proofreading what I wrote and gave me encouragement. My new fiance'e, Janet, gave me support, and boy, did I need it. My writing skills were raw, to say the least. Janet and I still laugh at one particular phrase that, at the time, I thought sounded pretty good. I had asked her and another friend, John Kratz, to proofread a section about agate distribution by glaciers. After reading what I wrote, they both sat silent, with smirks slowly forming on their faces. Pretty soon they burst out laughing. I could not understand what was so funny about agates being "dispersed more sparsely."

By the spring of 1986 I had most of the work for the agate book done. It was a good thing, too, because I had another big project to work on. Whenever I wasn't working, sleeping, or picking agates, I was preparing to get married. On May 31, 1986, Janet and I tied the knot. When we returned from our honeymoon in Hawaii, it was time to get serious about photographs for the book. I had acquired many beautiful specimens from George and others, and I began shooting away. Still a neophyte photographer, I knew I needed help. I was lucky enough to find fellow agate picker, Scott Poehler, who took agates I had found as partial trade for his photography work. We had a lot of fun taking those pictures.

The idea for the cover photo came to me in a dream one night. Janet and I took the photographs while standing atop Palisade Head a few miles north of Silver Bay, Minnesota. I had been there several times, and the view looking north along the Lake Superior shore to Shovel Point seemed like the perfect backdrop. Janet and I hit perfect weekend weather the day we took those pictures. She was standing pretty close to the cliff while holding that agate. Her bravery that day was for naught, however. We ended up having to transpose her hand, and the agate, onto the background photo. Regardless, we were both happy with how it all turned out.

At one point we were asked what we wanted to do for the back cover of the book. The wedding picture we ended up using made sense at the time. Janet had been so supportive through everything. The agates were involved in our courtship and engagement, so the photo seemed appropriate. Besides, for the people who didn't know us personally and had read the book, it let them know that we really went through with it!

In October 1986, we were ready to go to press. Don Harrer at Starr Press did a great job for us, and on November 10, I picked up the first boxes full of the *The Lake Superior Agate*. It's hard to explain the excitement of holding that first book with your name on the cover. I was happy and proud. It had been a long time since I felt that good about myself. The dark, guilt-ridden days over losing Dad were all but over. Endless hours of picking agates, working on the book, as well as the support of Janet, my friends, and my family had all helped to bring back the old me. I told myself that even if we never sold one book, it was all worth it. I will never forget my father, or that fateful trip, but I was finally ready to move on. And boy, did we!

It took three trips in my little red pickup to get all the boxes of agate books over to our apartment. I was surprised how big a pile 3,500 books could make. It was time to start selling them. My sales projections were based on very limited research and gut instinct. I figured that there had to be 2500 people who would pay money to read about Lake Superior agates. That was how many I needed to sell to breakeven.

I loaded up the truck and hit the road. I stopped at every gift shop, bookstore, and rock shop I could find, starting in the Twin Cities all the way up to Grand Marais. Amazingly, almost everywhere I stopped, people took at least a few books.

The freshly printed cover of the first *Lake Superior Agate* book. It was truly a thrill seeing a dream come true.

I also sent copies to local newspapers to try to get some publicity. Dave Wood at the Star Tribune in Minneapolis and Mary Ann Grossman at the St. Paul Pioneer Press both gave the book favorable reviews. I was on pins and needles when I read the review in the Lapidary Journal. Fortunately for me, June Culp Zietner, the queen of the rock-hound hobby, liked it, too.

Over the next couple of years, I worked hard getting the word out trying to sell the book. I was also asked to give slide presentations about Lake Superior agates, which gave me a chance to plug the book. We spoke to rock clubs, schools, professional groups, and anyone else that was interested in hearing about agates. Suddenly, I had become the "Lake Superior agate guy." I loved giving those talks. I'm sure people enjoyed the slides as well as the talk, but they couldn't wait to crowd around at the end and look at the agates I'd brought along. It was really fun to share these great specimens with people who could appreciate them. The talks were also a great way to meet other people who had collections.

Harold
Johnston

One of most important agate people I ever met was a man named Harold Johnston. The first time I met Harold was in the summer of 1984, shortly after George Flaim said, "You've got to see this guy's agates!" George explained how the two of them had played around with agates for many years and that Harold had a terrific collection. It didn't take much to get me lathered up, and within a few weeks, Janet and I showed up at Harold's door. He and his wife, Esther, graciously welcomed us into their beautiful, granite-stone lake home overlooking the northwestern Wisconsin town of Rice Lake. Harold was a well-built man in his sixties with a steely gaze and a warm, open demeanor.

As we toured the house, he pulled out a beautiful banded gem everywhere we went. He'd grab them off a shelf, out of a drawer, or from a display case in the basement. He had agates everywhere. Large ones, small ones, both rough and polished. Every specimen was a super. I realized very quickly that this guy knew what a good laker was. He also knew quality in many other things. Their home was filled with other beautiful treasures-paintings, unique furniture, and collectibles of many

Harold Johnston cradles the Foundation Agate next to Janet on our first visit in the summer of 1984.

kinds. It wasn't hard to predict that, even approaching retirement age, Harold wasn't slowing down with his rockhounding. He had a love of all rocks, minerals, and gemstones, but he had a burning passion for Lake Superior agates.

The first big agate that blew me away was the Foundation Agate. It was the finest big agate I had seen at the time. I could feel my pulse rate increase as he put it into my hands. I stole a quick "my gosh, I want this agate" glance at Janet, and she smiled back knowing exactly what I was thinking. A few years later, I eventually acquired the nine-pound monster from another collector that Harold had traded it to.

He had another big monster in the house, but this agate was only seven and a half pounds. It had an earthy reddish-brown color with a small, highly weathered, smooth quartz center broken up with a few floating bands. I later learned that the agate was found along a trail leading to the Buhl Iron Mine. George was familiar with the agate and told how the agate was found and then sold to Leo "Rocky" Quinn at the Beaver Bay Agate Shop. Rocky sold the stone to Harold. The agate was clearly much larger at one time in its geologic past, perhaps fifteen to twenty pounds. The remaining seven and a half pound "chip" was glacially eroded smooth with rich pastel colors.

Once we finished touring the house, Harold invited us inside his storage shed. I thought the "shed" would be a small rock room. It turned out to be huge, with a high ceiling and rows of storage shelves. Every shelf, walkway, and any open space was crammed with stuff. The shed was filled with all kinds of collectibles, but it was the rocks that I remember most. There were agates, minerals, petrified wood, and he even had a thousand-year-old bristlecone pine tree from California. Yes, the whole tree! He led us around and through the vast array of collectibles. There were piles of National Geographic magazines, machine parts, and bronze statues. Everywhere we looked we saw incredible things that he had picked up over the years during his many travels. Eventually, we found what we had come to see. He pulled a big laker from a cardboard box. It was a flat-shaped, four-plus-pound agate with reddish-brown color. It had a relatively fine-banded pattern that wrapped all the way around the edges of the stone. I call this type a sandwich agate and would I have liked to take a bite out of that beauty.

The next agate was an incredibly striking peeler with a huge, wide-banded face that weighed almost three pounds. The thick reddish-orange and white bands were separated with clear quartz. It was the finest example of a floater I had ever seen. Harold showed us many more fine gems that day, but it was those big ones that had my head spinning long after we left.

A few months after our visit, Harold learned that I was planning to write the first edition of The Lake Superior Agate book. He stopped by our apartment in St. Louis Park, and I'll never forget what he said; "I have the agate for the cover of your book." I remember thinking, "Yeah, sure you do!" Harold looked at me with quiet confidence; he knew what he was talking about. A few days later, he stopped by again and pulled out the eye-popping agate. It was a classic, fat-banded, red and white laker, the kind that collectors dream about. At almost exactly three pounds, it had it all-size, shape, color, quality, and pop! My skepticism about his bold prediction was instantly gone. Harold was right, and Janet and I knew it.

As I slowly regained my composure, the wheeler-dealer in me started to think. The collector part of me wanted all of Harold's big agates, but I knew he didn't want to sell them. If I could acquire any of them, it would definitely be this one. I made him an offer that I thought he would like. If I would include photographs of his agates in the book, would he would sell me the agate on the cover? He said it seemed like a fair deal, and we shook on it. We didn't agree on a price or put any timetable down on the sale. Harold was a deeply religious man, and I figured his word was good.

A week or two later, Harold dropped by again on one of his many trips to the Twin Cities from Rice Lake. He brought the agates I requested along with a special surprise, an expensive, large-format camera. I felt like a kid at Christmas. Huge, killer lakers and a high-quality camera to photograph them with. We spent several hours taking pictures that afternoon. Later that day, our discussion turned to other large agates that I might want to put in the book. Harold told me about a ten-pounder belonging to a friend that he thought he could acquire. "A ten-pounder" I said. "Where?" He said that it was very nice with red, orange, and white colors and very little quartz. The woman who owned it wanted $1,000, but he thought that was too much. It wasn't too much, in my opinion. I don't remember exactly what I said, but it must have been convincing. The very next day he showed up with something heavy in a grocery bag. Harold had a satisfied look on his face as I excitedly reached in and pulled out the dream agate. It was all of ten pounds, and it was a shocker! It was shaped like a tree stump with a huge, circular, banded face on the top. It was easily the nicest big laker I'd ever seen. Harold had blown me away again. As I cradled the precious gem in my hands, Harold beamed with delight. I think he realized it was a good investment after all. The 10.25-pound agate was reportedly found sometime before 1921 by a woman named Nina Cox. She believed until her death in 1981 at age 93 that what she had found was a petrified ham. It will be forever known as the Ham Agate.

While doing research on the book, I got a lot of help from Harold. Not only did he lend me his camera and any specimens I wanted, but he also introduced me to people he knew that had big, good-quality lakers. One of those collectors was a farmer in Forreston, Minnesota, named Bob Wiekert. Bob was a friendly, low-key guy who had a nice collection of Lake Superior agates, including a seven-plus-pounder. The agate contained a lot of quartz, but it had a nice shape and good color. That same day another friend of Harold's stopped by at the farm with a special agate he had found. Lyle Burghuis lived a few miles away near the town of Milaca. When I first saw Lyle's agate, I nearly had heart failure. It was a perfectly round, pill-shaped, dark red and white colored stone that weighed over six pounds.

The three big ones (left to right 9.04, 10.25, and 7.50 pounds) Harold Johnston had that nearly knocked me over.

It was one of the finest I'd ever seen. Harold had tried to buy the stone, but Lyle wouldn't let it loose. Several years later I would eventually talk Lyle out of it, but I would pay dearly for it!

When the book was finally printed, I couldn't wait to give a copy to Harold, with many thanks. Over the next couple of years, I worked hard getting the word out trying to sell the book. At the many slide presentations I gave, the agate on the cover of the book was always a big hit at show-and-tell time. I ended up having the Cover Agate more than Harold did over the next twelve years. We kept giving it back and forth whenever one of us had a talk to give or someone special to show it to. He was having as much fun as I was, or more, showing off that beautiful agate.

In 1993, on a trip to visit Harold and borrow the Cover Agate, I showed up at a very sad time. He was very upset, and he told me how his home had caught fire and was nearly a complete loss. I'll never forget walking through the house and seeing the damage. The water heater had ignited and burned a good part of the basement. I could see how the heat and smoke had roared up the stairs to the main level. The black soot on the ceiling tiles clearly mapped the path the smoke had taken pouring through the house. The upper level had escaped the flames by the time it was extinguished, but the smoke damage was extensive, and the smell was in everything. We looked in all the rooms and talked about how fortunate it was that no one was hurt. I remember seeing the tears well up in Harold's eyes as he pointed to the floor in one of the bedrooms. I could clearly see the soot-stained outline in the white carpet where their family dog had died.

We found the Cover Agate in the living room. It was covered with soot, but I knew underneath the black coating was the same pristine specimen. It had survived the heat from the fire. Harold gave me the agate and said, "I know you'll take good care of it." We went outside and got into his van to escape the cold. There I pressed Harold to sell me the agate as he had promised. This particular day felt like the right time to talk seriously about it. He told me that he wanted me to have it and that we had to establish a price. I was excited to finally talk business about the agate, but I could feel a lump grow in my throat at the thought of the eventual price. My jaw fell open when he said he wanted $10,000. Harold was a smart businessman. If I had had any doubts before, they were quickly erased. We wrote the dollar amount down on separate sheets of paper, and I left for home with the agate.

While driving home it became clear to me that our now seven-year-old deal on the Cover Agate was not going to happen. The value he put on the rock was more than I could pay, and was his way of saying that he was going to keep it. As tough a negotiator as I thought I was, I quickly realized that I had met my match. Harold had taught me a valuable lesson, one that I would not soon forget. A deal isn't a deal until the money changes hands.

Harold shared another personal setback with me on this visit. During our tour of the fire damage, we also looked at rocks in the storage shed. The big lakers I had seen on my previous visit, were stuffed inside winter hats, inside a large wooden box. On this visit, I picked up the same winter hats, and the big agates were gone. Someone had stolen Harold's biggest and best Lake Superior agates. He was obviously upset, and so was I. Not only for Harold, but for myself. In addition to the Cover Agate, I was hoping to eventually acquire some of the others. Harold's generosity and willingness to share his collection with others turned out to be too big of a temptation to some greedy thief. He said that other mineral specimens had also been taken, but whoever it was clearly targeted the big lakers. At least the Cover Agate had been in the house, so it wasn't taken. The incident left Harold shaken and angry. Sadly, his faith in his fellow rock hounds was forever changed.

Harold, with Esther along, was known for putting many miles on his van visiting his rock hound friends. At almost any hour of the day you could hear a knock at the door, and it would be Harold with his latest treasure. I never cared what time it was, because he always had something spectacular to show me. The last couple of years of Harold's life were pretty low-key in the rock-hound community. He didn't stop by the house anymore, but I would occasionally call, and we would talk about a recent find or purchase, or I would just ask how he was doing. He was always friendly, and the spark in his voice would still kick in when the subject turned to agates.

On April 14, 1998, Harold's son Darwin called to inform me that his father had passed away the previous day. He was eighty years old. The family put the Cover Agate on Harold's casket at his funeral. It was a fitting tribute. Even the theft of his most prized gemstones could never change his love of the hobby or the impact he had on others. I will always be grateful to Harold for his generosity and friendship. Even though a memorable character was now gone, his place in the history of Lake Superior agate rock hounds will always be secure.

Leo "Rocky" Quinn's Lake Superior agate collection at the Beaver Bay Agate Shop in Beaver Bay, Minnesota, in 1983. The biggest polished agate weighs over six pounds.

Fields of
Agates

As you can probably guess, I am repeatedly asked the same questions when talking to people about agates. Besides the inquiries about agate formation, types, and what to do with them, everyone wants to know where to find them. I usually respond by saying, "In people's basements." Which is really true when you think about all the beauties that I have bought or traded from other collectors over the years. However, what people really want to know is where they can collect their own agates. I give them the usual answers of rocky beaches, rivers, farm fields, gravel pits, and decorative rock within the Superior lobe glacial deposition area. In case you haven't realized it, I give vague answers to this question on purpose. Like any avid hunter or fisherman, I'm not going to tell anyone where my happy agate hunting grounds are.

It is fun to listen to people tell me about their agate-picking experiences. At the annual Moose Lake Agate Days show, I have ample time to meet many people, see their agates, and hear about how they found them. Usually, they talk about finding a big one after searching vast areas over a long period of time. This isn't surprising, since the big ones are usually few and far between. Every once in a while, I'll meet someone who shows me an incredible collection of large agates that they found over a relatively small area. Bill Boltz found a tremendous number of agates in specific areas in Topeka, Kansas.

We've speculated that perhaps the first Superior lobe glacier that passed over the birthplace of lakers sent an especially rich load of agate-filled debris south into Kansas. Before the first glacier came south into Minnesota, there was probably a long, quiet period of erosion. Lake Superior agates had over a billion years to

Oliver Hovda in 1997 with the amazing trove of agates he found near Austin, Minnesota.

erode out of the volcanic lava flows in which they formed. The area now occupied by Lake Superior was believed to have been a relatively rugged area with numerous rivers and streams cutting into the rocks. I've often fantasized about what it must have been like many eons ago. How hot would the fire be burning if you could go back in time and walk along those ancient stream beds? They must have been packed with agate nodules, although there would have been little or no banding showing since this was pre-glacier time. It would have been an agate cutter's paradise.

The relatively rich trove of those first glacial deposits appears to be present in Minnesota as well. On a late March afternoon in 1996, I was given a personal tour of one of these truly special areas. A warm sun was splashing down and melting away the final snowbanks of winter. I looked out the car window at the gently rolling farm fields as we slowly drove through this very special area. We were in southern Minnesota, not far from the "driftless area." Without the help of our gracious host, any chance of finding the area where an unbelievable collection of Lake Superior agates had been found was remote at best. I promised to keep the exact location a secret.

This area is located not too far from the town where our good friend Maynard Green lives. Maynard, however, is not the lucky individual who discovered this spot. This persistent, lucky man is Oliver Hovda. Maynard's longtime friend has farmed all his life just a few miles down the road from where he found his agates. It wasn't until Oliver was about fifty years old that he finally was able to put in serious time to collect agates. Oliver is a quiet, humble man, but when the subject turns to agates, he really lights up.

On this particular trip, fellow collector and friend Bill Steffes and I stopped by for a visit. It was a soggy Saturday in early spring, but the sun was shining through Oliver's living room window warming the room. The sunlight was pouring over the fruit of his twenty years of picking agates. This was the first time I'd seen all his agates together. It was an awesome sight. Bill and I immediately immersed ourselves as the proud papa looked on. There must have been fifty or sixty agates that were two pounds in size or more. Many were of nice quality, and about a half dozen or so were in the all-timer class. As I picked up each gem, I could feel that rush of adrenaline starting to surge. It had been a while since I'd seen a collection of that size and quality.

When we finally came up for air and turned our attention away from the agate pile, Oliver showed us his homemade fireplace that had many of his finds embedded in it. I asked him where he collected all these remarkable rocks. When he told us he found these agates in a roughly two-to three- square mile area, it was hard to believe. To our delight, he volunteered to give us a tour. As we headed down the gravel road and looked out over the fields, my mind tried to imagine what unique geologic conditions could have produced this special area.

It appears that Oliver stumbled onto one of those rare deposits from that first glacial lobe. I knew we were along the eastern margin of glacial debris in southern

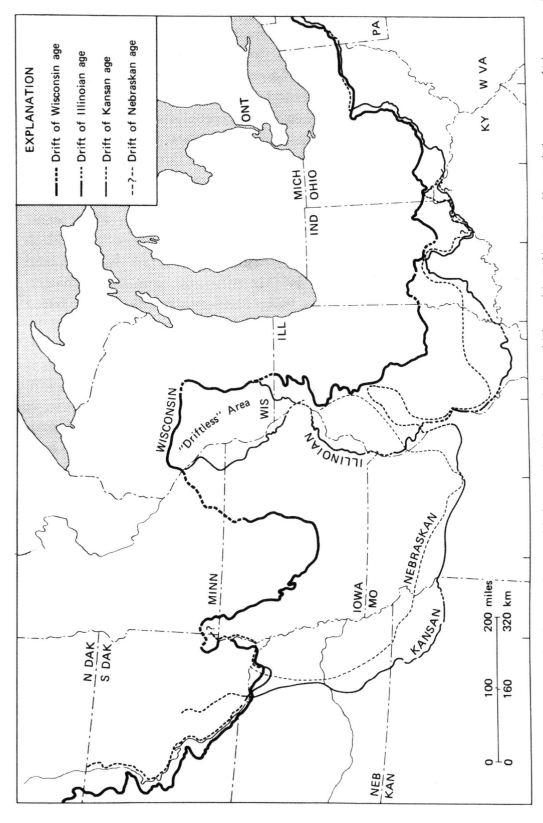

This map shows the maximum extent boundaries in North America of the four main glacial advances. Thin lenses of drift west of the "Driftless Area" could contain high concentrations of Lake Superior agates. (Reprinted from Flint, R.F. *Glacial and Quaternary Geology.* New York: John Wiley & Sons, 1971, pp.543.)

Minnesota, but without a detailed investigation of the local glacial geology, the exact reason for this agate hot spot is unknown. However, it seems reasonable to assume that the ice thickness and associated deposits along the margin were relatively thin. In fact, across the road from Oliver's farm is a large limestone bedrock quarry. The glacial cover in this area is only a few feet thick. This early, agate-rich lobe must have left a series of relatively large hills. Later advances must have deposited younger glacial material over most of the older debris, leaving only isolated pockets of the first lobe deposits.

The car slowed down each time Oliver pointed out a spot where one of his best big ones was found. Each time I had the urge to jump out and see if maybe one more was lying there. Knowing Oliver though, any agate that might have been there was picked up long ago. He explained how he would go agate picking on rainy days when the fields were too wet to farm. I chuckled and thought how convenient that must be.

Eventually, the tour was over, and Bill and I headed back to the Twin Cities. We talked about Oliver's amazing agates and wondered what special glacial conditions came together to produce this unique laker site. We also wondered where some other agate hotspots might be that have yet to be discovered. Maybe there are a few more Olivers out there that we have yet to meet. Either way, we both felt fortunate to have seen what from now on I'll call Hovda's hot spot.

Oliver Hovda in March 1996, standing where he found one of his best agates.

"Skonging"
Agates with Bruce Peddle

Bruce Peddle is one of those rare individuals who shares the same passion for lakers as I do and is an easygoing guy. Together we have acquired beautiful lakers in almost every conceivable way-purchased, traded, and picked them ourselves. Some of my most enjoyable moments with agates have been while doing shows with Bruce. For years we've shared a table at the Austin Gem and Mineral Show and parking spot at Moose Lake Agate Days. While picking agates together in gravel pits and farm fields, we've probably found close to the same number of agates each and we can both tell some pretty good agates stories. However, I have to say that Bruce definitely has me beat when it comes to finding big ones.

I first met Bruce at the Beaver Bay Agate Shop in Beaver Bay, Minnesota, in 1987. He had brought two big agates to show the shop owner at the time, Jim Haase. He had acquired them on his most recent buying trip. The agates were both around five pounds each, but not especially color-ful. They were, however, well-banded fortification agates with big attractive faces. One in particular caught my eye, and I asked if it was for sale. He said yes and asked me to make an offer. I said, "It's your agate, put a price on it." He probably wasn't too impressed with me, and said he wasn't ready to sell yet. Suddenly, I wasn't too impressed with him. After the stalemate over the agate, we talked about how he got them and he sur-prised me with what he said. He had driven over to the Little Falls, Minnesota, area and "knocked on doors." I said, "What do you mean, knocked on doors?" He explained how he would stop by farms in the agate-fer-

Bruce Peddle with a few of the bigger agates we "skonged" the day we bought the "Rainbow Paint" in 1993.

tile fields of that area and ask people if they had any agates they were willing to sell. As it turned out, most of them did! I had never heard or thought of this idea before, but it sure made a lot of sense.

After an hour or so, we each headed our own way. Even though I was a little annoyed about not getting the agate I wanted, I was impressed with Bruce's passion and drive. The more I thought about his method of acquiring agates, the smarter the idea became.

First, the Little Falls area is in the heart of the Superior lobe glacial deposition. Many beautiful agates have been found in this region of greater Minnesota-especially big ones. When the land was first clear-cut for farming years ago, the newly exposed fields were littered with glacial boulders and rocks. A practice began that continues today on most farms, the annual ritual of picking rocks from the field.

To spare the farm equipment from damage, the countless rocks littering the fields had to be removed. Most families had plenty of help from their children, who probably dreaded this laborious ritual of spring. One bright spot is that they must have found many Lake Superior agates. Just thinking about the number of farms with hundreds of acres of rocky fields is awesome. Imagine all the agates! When the children grew up and left the farm, the agates were usually put in the barn and forgotten. Most people considered the rocks of little value and were tickled to get any money for them. Eventually, I would experience this myself. Of the many people we saw who had agates, most were happy to sell, and many thought we were crazy giving them money for rocks. Some even refused our offers saying, "Here, take them."

As fate would have it, Bruce and I became fast friends. It was great to know someone with as much or even more passion for agates. Our first few buying trips together started by meeting in St. Cloud or Garrison, Minnesota, and then riding together in one car to go "skonging stone". Every time we bought a good one, we'd call it a skong. We skonged many good ones on those trips. The Rainbow Paint was one of them.

We were driving in my pickup one summer day, going north on Highway 169 between Milaca and Onamia. Bruce picked a dirt road to the west and said, "Let's go down that road." I turned onto the road, and after a couple of miles we passed by a farm field that looked like it had been recently turned over. It had rained hard the previous evening, and we could see clean rock everywhere. We decided to do a little picking of our own and pulled up to the farmhouse to ask for permission. Bruce jumped out and knocked on the door. An older man answered, and Bruce began talking with him. After a few seconds I saw Bruce look down. He bent down and picked up an ice cream bucket next to the door. He muttered a few words to the man and walked back to the truck with the bucket in hand. He opened the door, and when he put the bucket down on the seat I could see it was full of agates. Sitting on top was a huge concentric fortification face staring back at me. Dirty as it was, I could still see every color of the rainbow in the banding. I looked up wide-eyed at Bruce, and he said, "Give me twenty dollars, quick!" I couldn't get the money out fast enough.

The Minnehaha Falls Agate at critical points in its past. Native Americans surely felt as strongly about this amazing natural treasure then as we rock-hounds do now.

A sharp, rectangle-patterned shadow agate that pulls the viewer's eye to the center (10X).

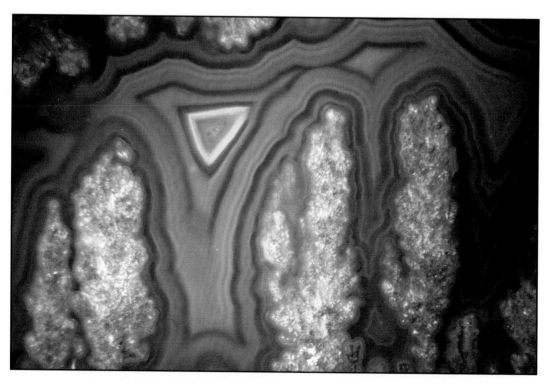

Organic-appearing hematite create plumes of iron oxide in this rarest type of Lake Superior agate (5X).

Dendritic growths of manganese oxide (pyrolusite) give the illusion of seaweed growing in the depths (10X). The dendrites grew between the parallel layers of a Lake Superior water-level honey agate.

Columns or stalks of iron oxide grow outward, toward the husk, from a lone white band (25X).

A "sunset" of radiating white sagenite deflects the subsequent forming bands (30X).
It appears as though the agate banding formed from the bottom up in this photo.

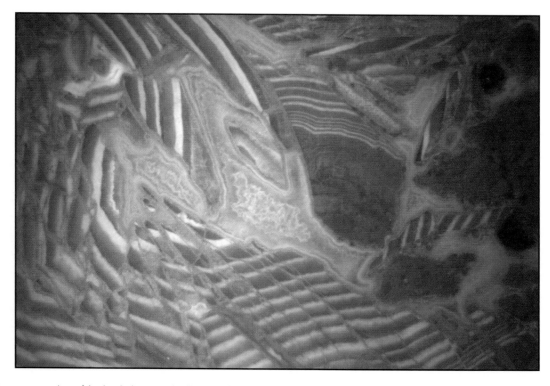

What was once a beautiful red and white agate has been transformed into a shattered mess from multiple generations of fracturing and rehealing (15X).

If anyone can tell me what's going on with this particular agate, let me know. A healed fracture, or ruin, clearly passes between the apparent broken band, which then loops backward at both ends (30X). Other bands appear to have broken but did not do the looping.

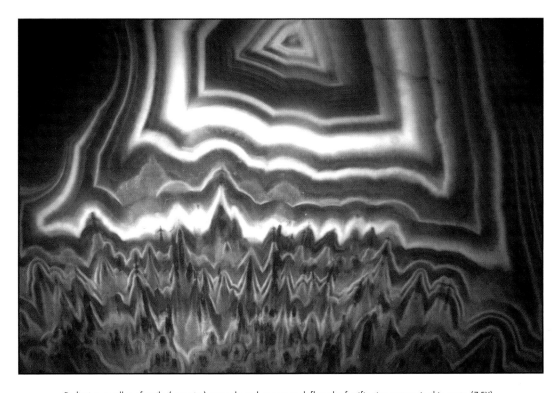

Radiating needles of rutile (sagenite) protrude and appear to deflect the fortification pattern in this agate (7.5X).

Two exceptional examples of sagenite agates. The two-pounder on the left has randomly orientated sprays of fine multi-colored rutile needles. The three-pounder on the right exhibits a large radial spray of needles that is complimented with various colored chalcedony.

Few polished lakers turn out as nice as this 0.98–pounder we call the "Bullseye Nodge".

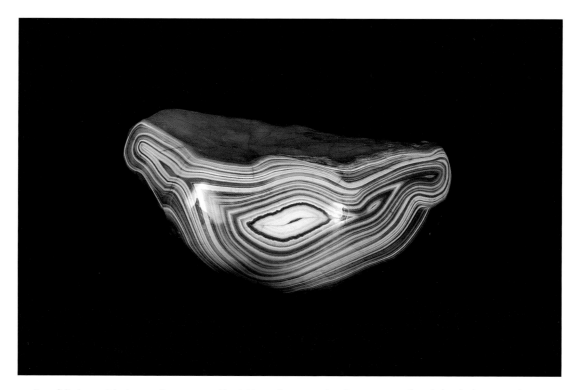

One of the best polished agates I've ever seen. This 3.83-pound agate was bought in a Minneapolis rock shop for $100 around 1970. The face was covered with yellow limonite which was ground off and then polished by Maynard Green.

At 5.25 pounds, this agate is the biggest high-quality polished Lake Superior agate I've ever seen.

While diving in about ten feet of water, I saw this beautiful agate from about twenty feet away.
It wasn't until I picked it up that I noticed the healed parallel fractures that extend into the basalt matrix.

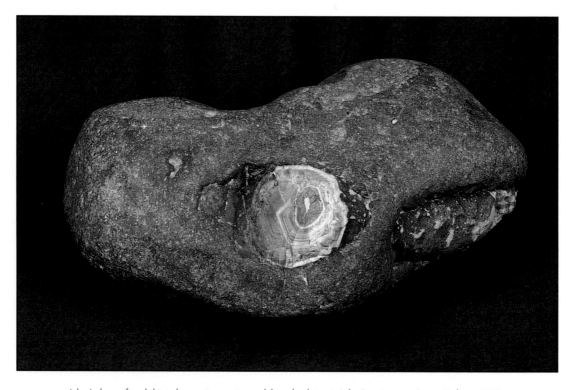

Jake Anderson found this truly amazing specimen while scuba diving in Lake Superior near Copper Harbor in 1999.
The roughly two-pound paint-stone is still embedded in the twenty-pound host basalt cobble.

When I peered in the window at the dive shop in Copper Harbor, this is one of the agates I saw.
Jake Anderson and George Twardzik chipped the more than ten-pound agate from the bedrock in Lake Superior in 1999.

This 11.44-pound monster paint agate was found a quarter mile inland while digging out weathered
basalt bedrock to make a lake near Copper Harbor, Michigan, in the spring of 2000.

The two agates Janet and Grant Wolter found while on a family agate-picking venture in June 2000.
Grant found the big one, a 1.75-pound paint-stone with floating bands.

Bruce Peddle found both of these agates (3.06 and 3.53 pounds) in a rock pile near Fort Ripley, Minnesota, on June 29, 1997.

The largest Lake Superior water-level agate I've ever seen.   This 4.10-pounder was found by longtime collector
Dick Pyle in a gravel pit near Cloquet, Minnesota, in the early 1970s.

A handsome collection of both rough and polished eye agates courtesy of John Harris.
Rarely over a few ounces in size, eye agates are the hardest to find and highly coveted.

Three, roughly one-pound agates with varying color and banding patterns.

A few of the better agates I found on the dredge in 2000. They range in size from 0.48 to 1.26 pounds.

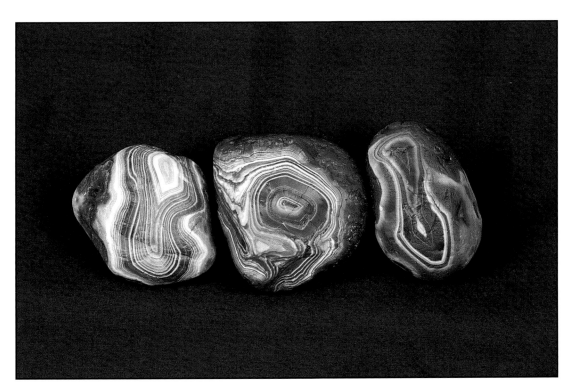

Three choice lakers from the Paul Hisdahl collection (left to right: 0.64, 0.95, and 0.50 pounds).

Three of my favorite agates from Harold Schmidt's collection that were all found in the Randall, Minnesota, area (left to right: 1.73, 1.68, and 0.98 pounds).

Dan Wiemer found these beauties, ranging in size from 0.50 to 1.75 pounds, in the southeastern Minnesota area in the late 1980s to 2000.

Jim Edberg found these dazzling beauties ranging from about one-half pound to a pound-and-a-half, while picking in the 1970s and 1980s.

Three of the better agates that Mike Pendzimas found in 1999 and 2000 (left to right: 1.83, 1.95, and 1.45 pounds).

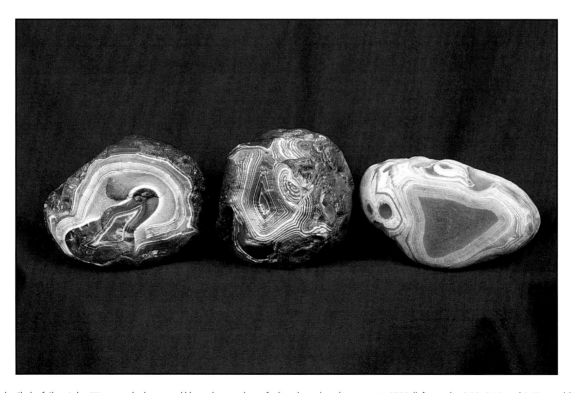

Charlie Clark of Clear Lake, Wisconsin, had an incredible twelve-month run finding these three big agates in 1999 (left to right: 2.25, 2.40, and 1.67 pounds).

A super half-pound, water-washed specimen Pat Malmsten found in 1995.

The beautiful banding, color, and contrast in this 1.29 pounder is highlighted by a perfectly smooth, wind-blown polish called ventification.

A farming family ritual of spring—picking rocks, and agates, from the field. (*National Geographic,* December 2000, pp. 100.)

He paid the man and jumped back into the truck. We pulled up to a puddle from the previous night's downpour and quickly washed the stone. The agate was relatively flat and probably weighed over two or three pounds at one time. It weighed only 1.25 pounds now. The husk on the back side was pink in color with no banding showing at all. The other side was all face. It was a paint-stone, rich in color with a "spider-web" fortification pattern. When we split up the agates at the end of the day, I ended up with the multicolored paint-stone. Before we headed home, we agreed on a name for it, the Rainbow Paint. Whenever someone tries to make a play for it, I just yell for my daughter, Amanda. She'll come marching down the stairs with that "Who wants it this time look" and pick up the stone. She quickly puts an end to any conversation about dealing on that one by saying, "This is my favorite agate."

Another memorable agate we skonged together is one of the largest glacial lakers ever. In the summer of 1998, I received a tip about a huge agate from a collector friend in Eau Claire, Wisconsin. John Harris, who specializes in making Lake Superior agate marbles, had actually seen this twenty-pounder the previous year. I thought I had seen all the big lakers and was a little skeptical when he told me the story. How many times had people called me about monster agates that turned out to be chert, jasper, or iron formation? Almost all of them. I have been on several agate wild goose chases and grown skeptical of giant agate stories. John, however, knew agates. If he said it was a laker, it probably was. He gave me the name and number of another rock-hound friend who knew the fellow with the rock. I called him, and he got me in touch with Nathan Horsch, who lived in Isle, Minnesota. Nathan said I should stop by the next day. I called Bruce and suggested we go see the agate together.

Bruce and I met at the big walleye statue in Garrison and headed for the town of Isle, on the other side of Lake Mille Lacs. We found the house less than a block from the lake. As Nathan carried the rock out to meet us, I could see it was the real thing. How many times had I let people down by explaining that the big rock they had found was not what they had hoped? This time it was a laker all right, and it was huge!

As he put the agate in my hands, I was overwhelmed by its size and weight. The agate was basically a quartz ball, but it was dense quartz with fine white banding swirling through every inch of the stone. The husk was completely spalled away with the exception of a couple of deep pimples. I could see smooth peeled areas and intermittent patterns produced by a wide white band that had been eroded by thousands of years of glacial transport. The agate was smoothly water-washed, and although not the solid monster-sized, high-quality agate people fantasize about, it was spectacular in its own right.

Nathan wasn't anxious to sell the rock; he'd had it for about ten years. His first job at age fourteen, was picking rocks for a farmer outside of Isle. He said he doesn't know who actually picked the rock up that day and threw it in the wagon. All he remembers is sitting on the wagon, taking a break, when he noticed the smooth spots (peeled areas) on a large rock. He thought it looked neat and decided to take it home. It wasn't until five years later that he learned from a friend at work, who was a rock hound, that it was a Lake Superior agate.

Eventually I convinced Nathan to sell the rock, and I promised to use it in the new book. We took some pictures, paid him, and jumped into the car. Bruce and I stopped at the first hardware store we could find and bought oven cleaner, a toothbrush, a bucket, rags and baby oil. We cleaned the agate in the parking lot, marveling at the size of the stone. It was a magnificent floater that ranks number two in size for glacial, nodular Lake Superior agates. We spent the rest of the day knocking on doors. I can't remember how many agates we got that day. All I remember is Bruce and I looking at the monster as we drove and laughing in disbelief. It was the rare time that the "twenty-pounder" turned out to be the real thing.

Nathan Horsch with his 19.87-pound monster agate the day Bruce Peddle and I stopped by in 1998. Nate was fourteen years old when he found the agate while picking rocks from a farm field near Isle, Minnesota, in 1988.

As tough as it is for "Mr. Competitive" to admit, Bruce has had better luck at finding lakers over two pounds than I have. He has earned every one of them. For years he has driven thousands of miles to comb farm fields, gravel pits, and Lake Superior beaches in search of trophy lakers. He found the Bozo the Clown Agate while looking out the window of his truck as he drove into a gravel pit. Like I did when I found Grant's Agate, he said he hit the brakes awfully fast.

I had the pleasure of witnessing one of Bruce's best finds. Early on a hot Saturday morning in 1985, I took Bruce to one of my favorite pits in the Twin

Cities area. The pit had been worked the previous day, leaving nearly vertical thirty or forty-foot high banks of clean gravelly sand. I walked along the top of the bank to head to a different area, while Bruce climbed down to search the recently worked bank. After a couple of minutes I heard him yell for me. I looked over the edge of the bank and saw him looking up at something. He said he thought he could see an agate. I walked over and looked down at the spot where he was pointing. I was closer to the rock than he was from my spot on top, but I couldn't see it. He tried to knock the rock out by throwing stones at it to no avail. Finally, he asked me to find a stick for him to dig it out with. The rock was at least ten feet over his head, so I knew I had to get a good-sized stick. I trudged off into some nearby woods and dragged out a ten-foot-long piece of wood that looked more like a small tree.

I threw it down to Bruce, and he reached up with it and worked the rock out. I watched from above as the nearly three-pound agate slid out from the bank. Bruce let out a yell and ran over to a nearby pond to wash it off. Needless to say, I scrambled down as quickly as I could to see his find. It was a red, white, and blue beauty. It was shaped like a long, flat hamburger, and I have to admit, I was a little envious. Any honest agate picker will tell you that he wishes he had found it. I really was happy that Bruce found it and that I had a small role in its discovery. A few hours later, at another gravel pit, I found a very nice blue, gray, and white 1.25-pounder. It was a very nice find, but a distant second to Bruce's rock that day.

Bruce's best day, however, was in the summer of 1997. He called me one day, excited about a new sorted rock pile he had found. It was in a gravel pit in the Little Falls area, with rocks up to the size of bowling balls. The workers at the pit told him the rock was to be used to line settlement ponds for a waste-water treatment plant.

Bruce Peddle proudly poses with the "tree" and his 2.77-pound beauty in July 1988.

I still kick myself for being too busy to join him when he asked me. I don't remember what was so important, but, boy, did I miss out. A week or so later, Bruce called, and he was giddy with excitement. A hard rain had washed the pile off, and I knew he had found something good. He excitedly explained that he had found not one, but two agates over three pounds! Knowing that it was a three-hour trip from Duluth to get to that pile, he had definitely earned them. I was happy for him. Both agates were well-banded, red, gray, and white trophies. Bruce's persistence reminds me of that old saying, "The harder you work, the better luck you have." Bruce is the hardest-working agate picker I know.

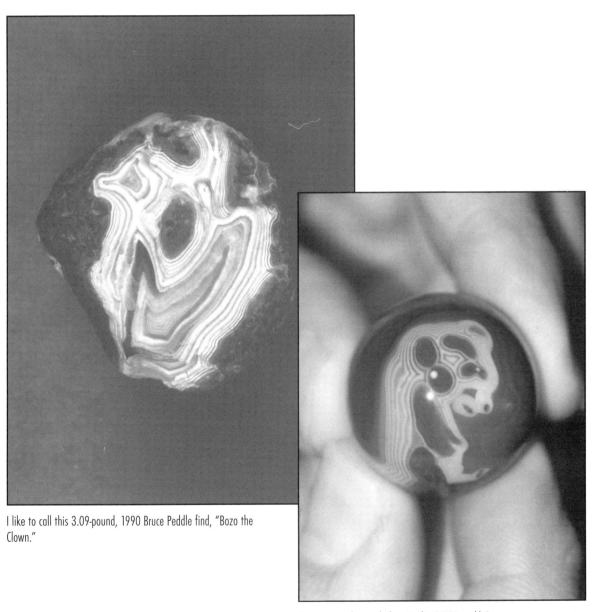

I like to call this 3.09-pound, 1990 Bruce Peddle find, "Bozo the Clown."

Can you see the panda bear in this 0.75" marble?

If you look carefully, an excellent image of "Abe Lincoln" will appear in this 3.31-pound water-level agate.

Some people see the storybook character "Curious George" in this 1.65-pound water-washed agate.

Picking Agates

As much fun as I've had chasing down and buying agates, there's nothing like finding them yourself. As I look back at my own history of picking, I can honestly say that I think I've done pretty well. I've found many great agates up to one pound in size, but only a couple over two pounds that were memorable for quality. To date, I still haven't found that big bomber red-and-white that would bring anyone who looks at it to his knees. But as anyone who has been out there looking for them knows, the all-timers are really tough to find. I know my day is coming, because there aren't many people who put more time and effort into looking for them then, I do. I've tried to make picking agates into a science, and every time I go out, it's another experiment.

For those who actively pick agates, the challenges to finding the good ones are many. The biggest challenge is finding a good place to go. I've talked before about decorative rock, construction sites, farm fields, gravelly river banks, and rocky beaches on glacial lakes as good collecting sites. The only place better to find lakers, other than another collector's basement, is in an active gravel pit. The good news is

I certainly enjoyed finding this 1.25-pounder while picking with Bruce Peddle on a hot day in early June 1988.

that there are literally thousands of gravel pits in the vast areas where Lake Superior agates are found. The bad news is that the people who own that property do not want agate collectors in there. The truth is, it's their insurance companies that don't want us in. The way life is today, people will sue anyone, for any reason, if they think they can get money from them. That's why we have such a difficult time. It's especially difficult in an urban area like the Minneapolis/St. Paul area where I live and try to pick agates. In spite of all the adversity, we will continue to persevere in the relentless pursuit of beautiful agates.

I've searched in gravel pits throughout Minnesota, Wisconsin, and even a few in Iowa, with varying success. By far, the lion's share of my picking time has been spent in the northern suburbs of the Twin Cities. The pits up there are loaded with agates, but they're also filled with agate collectors. The competition has been fierce for a long time. Throughout the 1980s and into the early 1990s, I fought it out like a foot soldier for my share. The bullets that shoot down the enthusiasm of even the most optimistic agate picker are footprints. There's nothing worse than finding a new sorted rock pile, or gravel-filled "drop," that has already been searched.

The late Jerry Barnett was a dedicated agate picker I used to see often in the pits. He was a big, strong, easygoing guy with a handlebar mustache. Whenever I ran into him, he was always smoking a long, thin Tipperillo cigarette, and walking very slowly. We would show each other what we had found, and he always surprised me. He certainly found agates, but he also kept anything that looked like an agate. If an area took me half an hour to look over, it took Jerry two hours. He was slow and methodical and didn't miss a thing. Whenever I went to a pit to pick, I always kept an eye out for footprints. It doesn't mean you can't still find something. I've found many agates in other people's footprints. But let's face it, your odds have instantly taken a nose dive. If I saw footprints *and* a Tipperillo wrapper on the ground, I'd turn around and go somewhere else. Any agate that might have been present in the pit was already in Jerry's pocket.

On the other hand, footprints can be used as a psychological weapon against your competitors. Many times I've found a great, freshly sorted rock pile or recently worked area with rock that is just too dirty to see anything. You can't help but think that someone will find this spot after you leave and beat you back there the minute it rains. To try and prevent this frustration, I've walked the virgin area or rock pile, leaving obvious tracks. The idea is to discourage whoever might beat me to the spot later on, when it finally does rain. Whether this trick actually ever worked for me, I don't know. But I have found good agates where I had previously left "phantom" footprints.

For a two or three-year period in the late 1980s, I had an agate-picking battle with someone who had relatively large feet. My favorite gravel pit went through a two-year period where the aggregate company was mining gravel out of a very large area. The front-end loaders were pulling out material at a frantic pace that produced seemingly endless stretches of high, steep banks. These banks were rich in coarse gravel that came cascading down and collected along the bottom. It was a picker's paradise with some of the best "drops" I'd ever seen. The day I discovered this dream situation, I vowed to make the most of it. I hit these pits hard, almost daily, for the first couple of weeks. Everything was going great. I was finding many good agates and, I'm sure, was on my way to finding the all-timer, when one day I saw them. They must have been at least a size twelve. I immediately looked up and all around, but didn't see anyone. Whoever it was, he had been there and left before I got there. To say I was disappointed is an understatement; I was mad. How dare someone else pick agates in my gravel pit? The first thing that went through my mind was what did he find? If he had found a big one, the only thing I could do was hope that it was full of quartz. I dreaded the thought that he might find the all-timer I was looking for.

The next time out, I went a little earlier in the day, and the footprints weren't there. "All right!" I thought. Now I could relax and enjoy myself. From then on, I kept wondering if this other person was thinking like I was. He must have been, because periodically the size twelves showed up again. This went on for weeks, but amazingly we never ran into each other. Neither of us knew who the other was. All I knew was that he had to be as frustrated as I was.

One day after finding a pretty good one-pounder, I decided to try and send "Size Twelve" a message. I made a small, but noticeable, pile of rocks. It was my way of letting him know that I had found a good one. I continued to build little shrines of rock to my rival, as a little agate ritual. I knew that if I got to the pit first, he wouldn't be long behind me and would no doubt see my little rock temples. Not long after I started this ritual, Size Twelve came up with one of his own.

An enticing wall of gravel I stumbled upon while picking in 1999.

Whenever I had to walk in his footprints, I started to come across big, quartz-filled agates sitting on top of a large rock, obviously placed there by Size Twelve. I think my little shrines had gotten to him. Every time I saw a big quartzy, it made me laugh. Whoever it was obviously had a sense of humor.

Eventually, we ran into each other. We laughed about how obnoxious our silly little rituals were. He turned out to be a pretty good guy, whom I had to respect. He had the same fire for agates that I did. Not too long after our meeting, the police kicked both of us out, and the agate wars at those pits were over.

A two-pound triangle-shaped dandy I found after a cleansing rain in 1987.

John
Marshall

1990 was an important year in my life in many ways. The most important event was the birth of our son, Grant. He is such a joy. All the cliche's describing the wonderful things about children, he is. I also left my job after four and a half years at Twin City Testing to partner with three coworkers and start a new testing company. It was a big step, but with these guys I knew it would work out. Eleven years later we're going strong and have never looked back. It was also the year that a lot of new discussion was going on about agate formation. Most of the talk centered around the so-called silica-gel theory, which basically states that open spaces, or vesicles, fill with silica from solutions moving through the rock. The silica gel then internally separates into bands via some as-yet-unknown mechanism.

This model is in sharp contrast to the other popular idea of agate formation called the multiple-deposition theory. In this model, each band is deposited one at a time, starting from the outside of the agate and moving inward. From the beginning, I have always leaned toward the multiple deposition idea. It always seemed to make sense to me. Whenever I carefully studied the agates I found, I never saw exactly the same thing twice. Banding pattern, iron content, and color were always

John Marshall holding three of his favorites during a 1997 visit. Obviously John didn't read the sign behind him.

different. Logic told me that each band had to be laid down individually. Other features I observed seemed to support the position I chose. Many agates had banding that had clearly separated, or peeled away, from layers underneath. I reasoned that this was due to a poor bond between the newly formed layer and the previous one.

Looking back, I realize that I had made my mind up early as to which theory I believed. From that point on, I was unwittingly biased and subconsciously looked for features that supported my position. Not very scientific of me, was it?

By this time I was in my early thirties and I knew for sure that sometimes I could be very stubborn. Once I made up my mind about something, it would take a lot to change this old mule's opinion. I also enjoy a spirited debate, the more controversial the better. The theory of agate formation was certainly controversial, but I knew very few people who could talk about the subject in any real detail. 1990 would be a turning point in my thinking of the way agates formed. This interesting odyssey began when I met a rejuvenated agate collector from Portland, Oregon.

John Marshall was in the Twin Cities visiting a friend that summer and wanted to get back into Lake Superior agates after a twenty-year layoff. He told me how he went into Berg's Rock Shop in Prescott, Wisconsin, and found my first book. He said it rekindled the interest of his childhood hobby, and he decided to give me a call. He said he was interested in seeing my collection and maybe buying some agates, so I invited him over. My first impression was that he was a very intelligent guy, but had I no idea how much he knew about lakers. I would soon find out.

That first visit was a lot of fun. We ended up talking a lot about the intricate structures in agates as well as exchanging ideas about their formation. It was definitely a spirited debate. John clearly supported the evolving vesicle-of-gel view, as if each agate had a life of its own. As he presented his spin on a particular point, I countered by pointing out features that were clearly in conflict with his model. Our many differences as people helped fuel our debates. John is a staunch conservative in his politics and has strong views about the Second Amendment in the Constitution. He was proud of his concealed weapons permit; I could care less about guns. As different as we were about many things, we shared the same strong views on environmental issues as well as our deep appreciation for Lake Superior agates.

John began making annual visits to Minnesota. We would always get together and occasionally take a road trip north to see George Flaim and other collectors. On a 1993 trip, we went to see John Kammerer of Minneapolis. John M. and I marveled at his rare Minnesota Iron Range minerals and fantastic polished Binghamite specimens. In over seventy-five years of collecting, John K. had also amassed many fine Indian artifacts as well as Lake Superior agates. Now in his late eighties and still very sharp, he was selling off his wonderful collection. John M. and I both picked up a few of John K.'s tumbled lakers that he had labeled and glued onto cardboard. I was also able to buy John's collection of National Geographic magazines. He had almost every issue dating back to April 1905.

Every now and then, I'll pick one out and read it. The ads in the older issues are the best. How about a fifteen-day cruise from San Francisco to Honolulu and back, aboard a luxury liner in 1910 for $110. That's in first class, of course!

John Kammerer poses with Janet during a July, 1989 visit. John collected Native American artifacts, rare Minnesota minerals, and Lake Superior agates for over eighty years.

It was on those road trips that John shared the stories of his youth with agates. He said his father was hard on him and his siblings. The only good memories he had with his father were his family's annual summer trips to the North Shore. He said they would hike down to secluded beaches and pick agates together. We also talked about how things have changed in agate collecting since he was last into it. John said they did a lot of cutting or, in his words, "slab 'em and cab 'em," in the 1950s and 1960s. I know I had an impact on him with my perspective of cleaning, oiling, and enjoying Mother Nature's work. It was easy to see that John was enjoying his second childhood after the long layoff.

Our friendship has been an eye-opener for me as well. "Mr. Stubborn" has had his strongly held opinions about agate formation challenged. I have not completely switched camps, but through John's persistence, I'm convinced that there is more going on than just one band at a time. We certainly haven't figured out all the answers yet. That will take many more insightful discussions with John and people like him.

Another thing about agates that John and I share is the emotional comfort we find pursuing our hobby. Collecting agates has helped both of us heal from painful experiences. I've come to realize that the rigid, hardball conservative from Oregon is really a big softy underneath. Give those pesky Lake Superior agates a chance, and they'll do it to you every time.

John Marshall's mother Mary searches for agates on a North Shore gravel beach in July of 1964.

Harold Schmidt

I can't remember exactly when I first met Harold Schmidt, but it was sometime in the mid 1980s. Someone had told me about the barber in Randall, Minnesota, who collected agates. One day when I was passing through the area chasing agates, I stopped into his shop and introduced myself. When I mentioned Lake Superior agates, he paused in the middle of a haircut and smiled. He pointed to a glass cabinet with a couple of nice specimens inside. I picked up the biggest one, which weighed about two pounds. It was polished on one side and had a beautiful cluster of bright red plumes surrounded with white fortification banding. I asked him where it had come from. He said the creek behind the shop flooded in 1972, and a couple of young kids found it along the bank. He chuckled and said, "I traded it from them for a couple of haircuts." I laughed and thought, "Whatever works." He said he had a lot more agates, and I should stop by his house sometime when he wasn't working. I took down his phone number and directions to his place and said I'd get back to him.

As things often go, it wasn't until 1991 that I was able to catch him. Bruce Peddle and I were passing through and stopped to see if he was home. As we walked up to the door, we noticed a small fountain in his yard that was made out of rocks, including slices of Lake Superior agates. We knew we were at the right place. Harold invited us in, and I immediately noticed his glass case in the middle of the living room filled with banded beauties. He had dozens of beautiful agates of all sizes, both polished and in the rough. The one that stood out in my mind above all the rest, however, was not one of the big ones. In fact, it was just under one pound and was only part of what must have been a much larger agate. The stone had tremendously bold and bright banding exposed on all sides, with rich red and orange oxidation colors. It was one of those lakers that would stop anyone in mid sentence and immediately grab their attention. I nick named it the Super Color Chip. As I scanned his case, my eyes kept gravitating back to it. There were other good ones in there, too. It was easy to see that they had a special place in his heart, and we weren't surprised when he said he didn't want to sell. It was still fun to see them, and I thoroughly enjoyed our visit. I left my card and told him if he ever wanted to sell, to give me a call.

Over the next several years I stopped by every time I passed through, but Harold was never home. It was a safe bet to guess where he was. Within one half mile of his house there were four gravel pits! Not only that, but he lives in a rural area with virtually no competition from other pickers. No wonder he was never home!

The next time I saw Harold was April 2000, when I talked to him about buying his agate collection. John Harris had recently stopped by to see Harold, who mentioned that he might consider selling his agates. While driving through the Twin Cities on his way home, John called to let me know about their conversation. Within the week, I was knocking on Harold's door. Another friend, Paul Hisdahl, rode along with me to see the collection and offer moral support. I would definitely need it if Harold changed his mind and decided not to sell.

Harold wasn't home when we arrived, but his wife Bea welcomed us in. The three of us chatted for a half hour or so until Harold came home. For the next two hours we talked about almost everything except agates. Eventually, the subject turned to our favorite gemstone, and I asked Harold how he first got into collecting them. He said he started picking agates in 1964 after a suggestion from his doctor. He had injured his back while in the military and needed to take some time off before going back to work. The doctor suggested several hobbies to fill Harold's time, and rock collecting sounded interesting.

When we went into his basement to look at his collection, it was obvious that he had been quite successful. There were several agates a pound and a half or larger on the bottom shelf of his case. They were as beautiful as I remembered, and I noticed that he had added a few big ones since my last visit.

When we started to talk about price, I could sense his mood changing. We had talked about his reasons to sell, but it was clearly a very emotional thing to let go of something that had been such a big part of his life. I certainly know how he felt. No amount of money can compensate for all the hours and memories those rocks represent. He said he felt like he was selling his children and, in a way, I guess he was. I really believe that knowing they were going to a good home made it easier for him. I told him he could stop by anytime he was in the Twin Cities and visit them.

We eventually settled on price, and I took some photos. As I was packing up the agates for the trip to their new home, Harold had a positive outlook. As he watched his case being emptied out, he muttered, "Well, now I'll have to get looking to fill that case up again." I told him when the case was full again, to call me and I'd be back!

Harold Schmidt poses with his Lake Superior agates the day he sold them in April 2000.

Big Bob

I think every good story needs a rival to motivate the central character. Throughout my agate adventures over the years, one person has done more to motivate me than anyone else. At first, we were less than cordial, due to the fact that he has as much competitive fire and passion as I have in the relentless pursuit of Lake Superior agates. But over the years and after numerous dealings, I came to understand and appreciate this dynamic individual, Bob Reineck.

I first met Bob at the June 1985 Minnesota State Fairgrounds Gem and Mineral Show. I was walking around the show looking at mineral and fossil displays as well as checking out the different dealers and their wares. I ran into a dealer I knew and struck up a conversation. While we were talking, another man walked up who also knew the dealer. The man appeared to be about my age, wore glasses, and looked like a football player. We were introduced and quickly started talking about our common interest, Lake Superior agates.

Bob talked about picking agates with his wife Lynn and some of the stones they'd found. My radar went up instantly when he told me about agates they had that were over a pound in size. I could tell that he knew a lot about lakers and clearly had a love for them. He and his wife were very friendly, and we made plans to get together. My hope was that he had some good specimens as well as an interest in trading agates or, better yet, selling them. I was to find out very soon.

The first time we got together he showed me some very nice agates. Two really stood out. The first was a red and white banded one-pounder with a cream-colored husk and a face that wrapped all

Amber Reineck poses beneath the 21.62 pound Counsell Agate, in the sure hands of her father Bob in 1991.

the way around the stone. Even though the agate wasn't huge, there was just something about it that I liked right away. The other was a three-and-a-half pound water-level that at the time was the largest of that variety I had seen. It had a dark, root-beer-colored husk with multicolored banding and crystalline quartz at the top of the parallel banding. Bob made it clear that he loved the agates, but that they could be had for the right price. I went home that night with the small one, still gasping at what I had paid. While haggling over price, Bob lamented how his wife had found the stone and that it was really hard to let it go. I couldn't tell if I had paid a premium for sentiment, or if Bob was just a good salesman. It was probably a little of both. I didn't bite on the big water-level on that visit, but I eventually got that one too. While driving home, I thought long and hard about this interesting fellow. He was clever and I knew I had to circle the wagons of strategy and figure out a creative way to work with this guy in the future.

Over the next fifteen years, Bob and I had numerous dealings. Many of those deals involved some of the greatest Lake Superior agates ever found. Fortunately for me, I was on the receiving end of most of those trophy lakers. Nearly all of the best agates I have in my collection I acquired directly from Bob, or at least he played a significant role in my acquisition of them. Not long after he sold me those first two agates, Bob decided to get into collecting in a big way. He once told me that he wanted his agates like he was-big! He wasn't kidding. Bob was right in the middle of what was literally the largest Lake Superior agate deal ever.

By December 1989, Bob and I had made dozens of agate deals. It seemed like every week one of us had dug up a new agate, and we always called the other first. One reason for calling was to try to one-up the other by bragging about the latest acquisition. Another reason was because we both could truly appreciate a fine stone and what it took to get it.

Usually I would be sitting at my desk at work when the phone would ring. "Announcement, announcement, I just got a nice agate!" My heart rate would instantly race up, and a quick shot of adrenaline would shoot through me. I know that he knew he was getting a rise out of me, the jerk! Bob confessed years later that whenever I called him with an "announcement," he had the same reaction. I always put away whatever I was doing and gave him my full attention. "How big is it? Is it a nice one?" I'd hear that sinister chuckle on the other end of the line, and then a short pause. "Do you want to make a deal, Scott?" The answer was always yes, and we'd make plans to get together, usually that same day.

This particular day happened to be December 21, my thirty-first birthday. By this time, Bob had assembled some pretty impressive big lakers in his collection. There were several that I would love to have had, but there were two in particular. One was the nine-pound Foundation Agate that he had traded from Harold Johnston.

The other was an eight-pound, solid nodule we called Big Blue. This agate was slightly elongated in shape with a relatively small face of thick, white banding on one end. It's large size, complete nodular shape, and beautiful light blue color make the stone particularly attractive. Big Blue has a colorful history that started sometime before 1930. It was found in a farm field near Hinckley, Minnesota. Reportedly, it was used to pay for dental work sometime in the 1950s. Several years later, the agate was sold to George Flaim. George sold it to Albert Peterson in

Foley, Minnesota. Albert ran a gas station in town for many years and had a large collection of various types of agates, including lakers, in the back of the station. All the rocks were in glass cases that made his collection look like a small museum. Bob had traded for the big agate from Albert earlier in the year and was now offering it to me.

Bob showed up at my office with the big agates and set them down on my desk. He sat down with a big smile on his face. As I looked at him, my emotions were churning. I was excited knowing I had an opportunity to acquire not one, but two fantastic stones, but another part of me was sick at what I knew was going to be a stiff price tag. I swallowed hard and said, "So, what do you want for them?" I braced myself as he opened his mouth and said "$7,000 for both of them." Once I got over the initial shock, it wasn't so bad. My mind immediately went into agate justification mode.

That was $3,500 for each rock. Sure, it was a lot of money, but how often does a chance like this come along? Besides, I can make more money down the road. I've bought many agates that were worth more than what I paid for them, so it all evens out in the end, right? I knew what the answer

Albert Peterson seated in front of part of his Brazillian agate collection in 1988. Albert had an agate museum that included many beautiful lakers behind his gas station in Foley, Minnesota.

was before I even asked myself the question. "Let's do it, Bob." We did the deal, and he quickly left with that smile still stuck on his face. I went home that night with a big smile on my face, too. This was one of the most memorable birthdays I had ever had. Little did I know that this was only part one of the deal. Before I got home for my birthday party, on a twenty-five-degrees-below-zero night, Bob was already on his way to Duluth. He was after an even bigger prize.

The 21.62-pound Counsell Agate is still the biggest nodular Lake Superior agate ever found in glacial drift. In 1988, the Counsell Agate was sold, in a silent bid, to a fellow named Gary Thompson, of Duluth. Bob had already agreed on a $7,000 price for the big agate, and now he had the money. The day after our big deal, the phone rang again. "Announcement, announcement!" I couldn't believe my ears.

What could he possibly have now? It didn't take long to find out. Bob came strolling in like a proud papa with his brand-new baby. I recognized the Counsell Agate immediately. That son of a gun had done it. He had skonged the biggest laker of them all. That smile on his face said everything. As I sat there and listened to his story of the frantic night before, an idea suddenly popped into my head. One of the reasons that we pursue these prize agates is for the satisfaction of showing them off. There's no greater thrill than sharing a prize agate with someone who can truly appreciate it. I knew this fact would help sell a practical joke that I couldn't resist trying.

I asked Bob if I could quickly show his big agate to somebody in another office. "I'll show it to them real quick, then I'll be right back." With a satisfied smile, Bob said, "Sure, I'll wait right here." I walked out with the big agate and went into our concrete testing lab. I quickly told a couple of coworkers about my plan, and they agreed to play along. Practical jokes were commonplace at my office, and they were eager participants. I asked if I could borrow a concrete cylinder. These cylinders weigh about thirty pounds and would work perfectly for my little prank. I went back to my office and placed the big agate quietly on the tile floor near my office door, just out of Bob's eyesight. I backtracked down the hall with the concrete cylinder and my coworkers. On cue, we started toward my office talking loudly so Bob could hear us. As we approached the door, I stopped, put my foot on the agate, and threw the concrete cylinder down the hall. As the cylinder crashed loudly out of sight, I let out a loud "Oops!" and gently, with my foot, slid the agate across the opening of the door. I knew Bob's blood pressure would immediately shoot up, thinking his precious agate was crumbling to pieces because of my apparent clumsiness. When we peered around the doorway, Bob's face was ghostly white and his mouth was hanging wide open. My friends and I laughed for ten minutes before Bob finally composed himself. He looked at me with that "I'll get you back someday look," and in a good-natured voice said, "You got me!"

Practical jokes and one-upping the other for agates; for years that's how it was with Bob and me. The competition between us for agates was fierce. We both frantically followed the smallest leads to find the next collection or big specimen. We often called to try to figure out what the other was up to or to catch up on the latest agate gossip. We drove each other nuts by teasing about a good agate we were working on. Bob's way of trying to figure out what I was doing was by asking a lot of questions. He tried to be subtle, but I knew what he was doing.

If I said I was going south to look at a big agate, he knew the lead was somewhere up north. As silly as it sounds, I often used Bob as a mental motivator. Whenever the leads went nowhere, or a person with a good one did not want to sell, frustration would set in. Quitting was never an option, of course. All I had to do was think about what Bob might be doing, and I would quickly get on my horse again.

Another fact of our agate life that kept both of us on our toes were the leads that we both already knew about. There were several that had to be continually monitored. This way we kept whatever foothold we thought we had, real or imagined. Every once in a while, however, a secret lead on a nice big agate would be exposed. "Yeah, there was this big fella named Bob who stopped by and topped your offer on the agate."

After the initial shock, my surprise quickly turned to anger. It was a great personal challenge, trying to maintain my composure while doing a slow boil on the inside. I'm sure the owner of the agate knew exactly how I felt and was happy that they had more than one suitor for their stone. One of those trophies that we were both after was the Berghuis agate.

After Harold Johnston introduced me to Lyle and his big agate, I told myself that I would not say a word about it to anyone. For the first couple years I felt secure. Lyle wasn't ready to sell, and I was content to let the agate sit until I came up with a workable deal. I didn't know when an opportunity would present itself, but it was obvious that patience would be necessary with Lyle. The only thing I knew for sure was that if Bob found out about this one, he'd be all over it.

At the 1990 Moose Lake show my little agate secret quickly became front-page news. I was sitting at my table selling books and agates in the parking lot when Big Bob wandered over. He said hello in a rather sly way and said he had something to show me. He pulled his hands from behind his back and shoved the familiar agate into my face. Bob had borrowed the agate from Lyle to chastize me. Besides my obvious disappointment, I realized that if I ever was able to get the agate, it was now going to cost me more-a lot more. A short time later, Lyle walked by and said, "Bob made me a nice offer; it sure is good to know that other people are interested in the agate." Biting my lip, I grudgingly agreed and said I'd be back in touch. Over the next four months, Bob and I went back and forth with Lyle, each of us trying to pin him down to a price. The whole thing eventually came to a head when a third person stumbled onto the agate.

On a cool November day, the phone rang at work. I picked it up and it was Lyle. He said that somebody was at his home trying to buy his agate. Panic quickly set in when I realized that the reason he called was because he was probably ready to sell. I asked who it was and he said that the person didn't want him to say. I thought of Bob right away. Lyle said that the mystery person had topped my last offer, and he wasn't sure what to do. In other words, "Will you top this offer?"

Lyle had us right where he wanted us, in a bidding war. My mind started racing with emotions trying frantically to think of what to do. It was driving me crazy knowing someone was standing there, ready to walk off with the agate I had worked so hard on for so long. I had to come up with something fast. One thing I had on my side is that Lyle and I had known each other a fairly long time and had mutual respect. If not, he wouldn't have called me. Eventually, an idea came to me.

I said, "Lyle, if we can agree to a price, will you sell the agate?" He hesitated and said, "Yes, I guess so." "OK," I said, "tell that other person to write down on a piece of paper their final offer." Lyle hesitated, I'm sure realizing that this would stop the bidding war that he had enjoyed for the last six years. I said, "Go ahead, tell him to write down his final offer." He said, "OK," and put the phone down. I sat there riveted, straining my ears trying to hear the voices in the background. I was dying to know who the mystery person was and what his final offer would be. In a way, I was playing agate Russian roulette. What if he bid higher than I was willing to go? By pinning Lyle down, I may have been cutting my own throat.

After what seemed like an eternity, Lyle came back to the phone. He said, "I have the paper here." I said, "Open it up and read it." I could hear the paper rustle, and he said, "$5,700." I gasped a little, but not too bad. My next words were, "Lyle, if I beat that offer, will you sell it to me?" I could hear him swallow hard and say, "Yes." I agreed to pay $5,800 and said that I would call back in a half hour, after his mystery buyer had left. I put the phone down and let out a huge sigh of relief.

When I called back, he said the prospective buyer had left and was not very happy about what had just transpired. When Lyle finally told me, I was shocked to learn that the mystery person was not *Big* Bob. It turned out to be somebody I didn't even know.

A few days later, after I picked up the agate, I made the customary "announcement" call to Bob. When I told him about the Burghuis agate he said, "I knew you got it." When I asked him how he knew, he said he had given the lead to the mystery buyer and sent him up there. He said he figured that the agate would command too much money for him so he wanted to "stir the pot." He stirred the pot all right. As it turned out, I should probably thank Bob. His little prank was what finally motivated Lyle into making a decision.

Even though Bob and I spent years as agate rivals, we always had a healthy respect for each other. Bob outdid himself time and again with trophy lakers he pulled out of the woodwork. One thing I have to thank him for is the opportunity to buy most of the really great agates he dug up. The "announcement" calls from Bob were always bittersweet. I knew that whatever agate he had would be good, and I always tingled with anticipation to see how good. The downside is that he never had discount prices on his hard-earned specimens. It didn't matter though; almost all the agates he came up with were worth the money-even if I didn't have it. This is a classic symptom of the advanced stages of the dreaded Lake Superior agate disease.

Like many nonessential but highly desirable things in life, the good agates always come along when you can least afford them. For non afflicted individuals, common sense kicks in. They do the math and say, "Not right now." When the flames of agate fever flare up, your brain starts rationalizing the facts so that they add up to another agate purchase. First, the rarity of a super-quality, big agate is undeniable. All I have to do is think about how many miles I've walked and how many footprints I've seen trying to find them myself. Justifying the rarity is easy; justifying the money takes more work.

After cringing at Bob's prices, I figured out early that he always started off asking for the moon. It was up to me to make sure that somehow we met back on earth. It is always hard to figure out how much the seller needs the money. The more the money is needed, the easier it is to deal. Whenever I found myself negotiating with Bob, I knew the need had to be somewhat serious. Because of his love of lakers, his decision to sell meant the need was stronger than the want. This fact certainly worked in my favor.

On the other side of the coin, Bob had cards in his hand. There were definitely other collectors interested in his agates, and probably all of them he'd rather spend time with. He realized that somehow I always came up with the money. But the ace in his hand was the card I played for him. My insatiable appetite for agates was my downfall. The better the agate the more Bob knew he had me.

In the end, I'd always say something like this to myself: "This is a rare and beautiful agate. . . . I've never found one this big or this good, probably never will. . . . Besides, I can always make money, this agate will not come along again." Sooner or later, I always went home with a new treasure.

After ten years of beating each other's brains out for agates, we eventually agreed to a truce. The cease-fire was reached during a long road trip to Topeka, Kansas, in October 1993. I invited Bob along on a mission I knew he'd enjoy. Long time collector Bill Boltz had recently passed away, and his family generously agreed to donate part of his collection to the state of Minnesota. Eventually, the agates will end up on display in the Agate/Geological Interpretive Center in Moose Lake. I had the privilege of representing the state to select and then transport the agates back to Minnesota. Bill had such a large collection that three lucky recipients each received a generous share of agates.

I didn't know if Bob would be interested, but he enthusiastically accepted my invitation. To my surprise, I had a lot more fun with him than I thought I would.

Bill Boltz and his wife Helen between Janet (pregnant with Grant) and Mike Carlson during a 1990 visit to Topeka, Kansas. Bill donated parts of his tremendous collection of Lake Superior agates to universities in Missouri and Kansas as well as to the state of Minnesota.

The whole way down we talked about everything that was agate. I found myself laughing out loud at hearing his side of the story to our numerous encounters. After eight hours we arrived at the Boltz home. In addition to the State of Minnesota, The University of Kansas in Topeka sent a representative who had already selected their portion of the collection. Even so, we were able to pick out a beautiful collection of agates. The next day, on the ride back, we had even more fun. We both told agate stories, only this time we had a car full of banded beauties to enjoy them with.

When we finally rolled back into the Twin Cities, I had a different perspective on my agate competitor. I learned many things about this guy. Bob is a great storyteller who had me roaring several times with humorous insights on collectors we both knew. I also saw how clever he was at obtaining leads and tracking down agates. While listening to him talk about his agate pursuits, I began to figure out why he didn't keep the fabulous agates he acquired. For Bob, it was the thrill of the hunt, figuring out where they are and how to get them. He said for a long time it didn't matter to him where the agates went, as long as he got his money. Once the safari was over, it was on to the next one. Over time though, he said his thinking began to change. He confided that he eventually came to appreciate that if they were all together, at least once in a while he could see them again. I think that was another reason why he sold many of his big agates to me.

Even though he didn't keep his acquisitions very long, Bob's role in their history cannot be denied. He's one of the few people with the agate fever bonfire that burns as bright as mine does. When I sat back and thought about it, I felt fortunate to have done battle with a worthy agate gladiator.

Bob Reineck acquired these two monster agates (8.93 and 11.96 pounds) the same day on a buying trip to Iowa in 1991.

The Ham Agate

Another subject Bob and I talked about on the trip to Topeka was Harold Johnston's stolen agates. We felt it was demoralizing and tried to figure out which ones were missing. We also wondered who might have taken them. Bob and I both knew Harold well, and we had both seen the big agates in the winter hats. They were all great pieces, but we agreed that the one we'd miss the most was the Ham Agate. I listened with a heavy heart as Bob described how he thought it was the best big agate ever. From the day Harold first showed it to me, it was the best big one I had seen, too. It was on loan at my house for almost three years, and I feared I might never see it again, much less get a chance to acquire it.

Bob shared his disappointment that some people thought he was involved in the agates' disappearance. Bob was a colorful character, but stealing agates from a long-time friend was just not his style. It was five more years before the mystery was solved.

In May 1999, I called Bob Lynch, the owner of the Agate City rock shop in Two Harbors, Minnesota. He had recently returned from Rice Lake, Wisconsin, where he had purchased the entire Harold Johnston Lake Superior agate collection, with a few notable exceptions. He told me about how many agates Harold had and how many days it took for him to go through it all. I had seen the fruit of over thirty years of Harold's agate excursions, and I laughed to myself thinking about what a job that must have been. Bob's arms and back had to be sore from lifting the never-ending boxes and buckets of agates.

Agate collectors come in many types. Some look only for big agates, others collect different types. Many want only red-and-whites, others like the pretty paints. Harold was a collector who loved every type, no matter how big or small, attractive or not. He wanted whatever he could get, and over the years he got a lot of them. Harold wasn't a guy to spend hours setting up displays for his agates; he simply stockpiled them. He was always more than happy to show people his voluminous collection or latest acquisition-if he could find it. No wonder it took Bob several days to find them all.

Bob was obviously pleased to have a new trove of agates to sell in his shop. He did, however, express frustration at not being able to buy the biggest and best ones. I asked him why, and he said that Esther and the four children had decided to keep several of the nicest ones. He said he had seen and appraised them all. I was curious and asked him to describe the ones he saw. My mind went wild trying to picture what each stone looked like as Bob described them. I suddenly perked up when he said, "There was another one that was about ten pounds." "Ten pounds," I said, "Tell me what it looked like." As Bob began to describe it, I couldn't believe my ears. The picture that emerged sounded awfully familiar. The last thing he said was, "It looks a lot like a ham." My jaw nearly hit the floor. The Ham Agate was still there.

Suddenly I realized what must have happened, or rather, not happened. I excitedly starting quizzing Bob about what else he saw. It turned out that all the agates that everyone thought had been stolen were still there. It appears that Harold had simply misplaced them. With all the things that he had stuffed inside that building over the years, it's no wonder they got lost.

My heart raced with excitement and relief. Since all of Harold's best agates were still there, it meant they might also be available for purchase. Since Bob had worked closely with the family and bought all of the lakers he was able to, he figured he had the best shot to buy the good ones they still had. He said they weren't ready to sell them at the present time, but when they were, he'd get them.

Over the next several months, many Lake Superior agate suitors pressed the Johnstons to sell the good lakers. The agate inquired about most was, of course, the Ham Agate. Each time, however, they were turned away. I made my own inquiry, but I was also rejected by the family and joined the other jilted collectors. It seemed that Harold's habit of holding tightly onto his treasures had been passed on to his children.

At just about the time I thought no one would be able to wrestle any of those agates away, someone did. Our boy with the magic touch struck once again. By the end of the century, the fervor over the Johnston agates was beginning to die down. It was a couple of weeks into the new millennium when I received a phone call. When I heard big Bob's voice, I realized I hadn't spoken to him in quite a while. Whenever he was quiet in the past, he was usually working on something big. The voice, speaking a little quicker than usual, said, "Announcement, announcement." I laughed and said, "Where the hell have you been? Bob said, "Scott, you're not going to believe it; I bought the Ham Agate." He was right; at first I couldn't believe it. I thought, "How could he get it when nobody else could?" I know he had pulled a rabbit out of the hat getting agates before, but this time he had outdone even himself.

"Bob, how the heck did you do it?" I sat back and listened to how the master skonger landed the top prize. He told me he bought it three weeks earlier, on December 26. He said he knew they'd be home and added, "Do you know what people are doing the day after Christmas? Nothing." He showed up with his wife, Lynn, and the best motivator there is, crisp hundred-dollar bills.

He told them how he had been accused by many in the rock-hound hobby of stealing Harold's agates. He said his reputation had been damaged. Now that it was clear that the agates were never stolen, he finally felt vindicated. He asked Esther if he could buy one of the big agates to keep as a memento of his friendship with Harold. The one he wanted was the one that mattered most.

With two of her daughters present, feeling obviously mixed emotions, Esther told Bob to take the agate he wanted. She insisted he pay her the price that Bob Lynch had appraised it at earlier. She apologized for the misunderstanding about the "stolen" agates and said she hoped a wrong had been made right.

Once again Bob had come up with yet another awesome specimen. He was able to do what no one else could. In the old days I would have been painfully envious, but this time I was genuinely happy for him. For almost seven years he had been the object of suspicion. I have to admit there were days when I wondered if he knew something about the missing agates. Another reason I was happy is that if I was ever to have a chance at that agate, Bob was my best shot. If anyone else had acquired it, I could have kissed it goodbye forever. When he told me about the rock, my first instinct was to immediately start working on him, but I stopped

myself before I even started to think about it. I thought, "Let the hunter enjoy his trophy." Experience told me that I needed to be patient. For once I decided I would be.

I congratulated him and said I could hardly wait to see it. He told me I was the first one he called to tell about it, and that meant a lot. The next day he came by my office to show it to me. It was the first time I had held the magnificent giant in almost ten years. The rich, orange-red color of the husk glistened in the bright sunshine. The tightly banded, bull's-eye face protruding out the top explodes with color and quality. It is, without question, the finest quality big Lake Superior agate of them all.

Before Bob left, I told him to have fun showing it off to all our agate buddies. I also told him that when he was ready to sell, to give me a call. On May 3, 2000, it was my turn. We met in the parking lot at my office, and I climbed into his car. Bob looked over at me and stuck out his hand. I reached

Amanda Wolter with the Ham agate in May 2000.

into my bag, pulled out a bundle of bills and slowly counted them out. It seemed like an eternity for me, but it all went quickly for him, I'm sure. When he put the brute into my hands, I felt as though a long journey had come to an end. For a die-hard agate fanatic, it was like winning the Super Bowl of Lake Superior agates. What a rush to finally have it!

There is no question I am happy to have not only the Ham Agate, but all the rest of the beautiful agates in my collection. However, it is important to put things into their proper perspective. The time I have to own these fantastic treasures is but a millisecond in their history on this earth. They have already been around for over a billion years and will still be here, hopefully, in a billion more years. I believe there is a responsibility that goes with owning these magnificent stones. I hope future rock hounds will welcome that responsibility and, as George Flaim once said, "Pay respect to all lakers."

Moose Lake
Agate Days

I first heard about the Moose Lake Agate Days Gem and Mineral Show in the spring of 1984. For someone stricken with agate fever like I was, this show sounded like the perfect fix. I had already been to a couple of gem and mineral shows and thoroughly enjoyed them. As fun as those other shows were, this one sounded like the ultimate agate experience. I couldn't wait.

On a hot, mid-July morning, I pulled my car into the school parking lot, but all the spots near the entrance were filled with people sitting behind card tables. Scattered on the tables were Lake Superior agates. Once I found a place to park, I excitedly checked out what these people were up to. They were agate pickers selling the rough specimens they had collected. There were many nice agates on each table and I thought it was a great idea.

After my initial sweep of the tailgaters, I went inside the school to see the "real" show. The gymnasium was filled with dealers selling rocks, gems, and jewelry, but relatively few Lake Superior agates. I did, however, see one stunning rough agate inside a display case that I later learned was for sale. It weighed about two and a half pounds and was far better than anything I had seen outside. The agate had bright red, white, and blue colors and belonged to a local guy named Tom Olson. Tom was one of the founders of the Moose Lake show and told me he found the agate in 1958. He said he was loading gravel into a truck when it showed up on the end of his shovel. Once I realized that it was available, I went into agate acquisition mode. I asked Tom for the price, and he said he had been offered $300. The beauty of the agate overcame my fiscal judgment, and I offered $400. Tom raised his eyebrows at my offer, and by the end of the show, I was the proud new owner.

Years later, George and a couple of other collectors who were there said that, at the time, they thought I was crazy to pay that much money. Now, the price I paid for the Patriotic Agate would be a bargain. It was a memorable first experience, and I haven't missed a show since.

In January 2001, I had a chance to visit with Tom Olson about how the show got started. He told me he attended the Duluth Gem and Mineral Club show at the Kenwood Mall, and decided to get a show going for the Carlton County Rock Club. After months of hard work by Tom and members of the club, the first show was held in the summer of 1969. He said the show was held outside on picnic tables, and it rained the whole time. The city invited the club to bring their display cases into the city museum and let them present their slide programs in the theater.

Tom also relayed how he and Jean Dahlberg lobbied at the state Capitol to have the Lake Superior agate designated the Minnesota State gemstone. The competition lobbied hard for pipestone and Thomsonite, but in the end, our gorgeous agate was selected. Tom said he gave out 340 polished lakers to legislators and senators to help educate and arm-twist. He also gave then governor Harold LeVander a Lake Superior agate tie tack cut into the shape of the state of Minnesota. Tom has been at the helm ever since, piloting the show through continued growth and great success.

One of the things that make Moose Lake Agate Days special is the tailgaters. Other gem and mineral shows have dealers, displays, and presentations. Only Moose Lake has the rough-agate peddlers with their recently discovered specimens, fresh from the pit. I am a regular tailgater myself at the show, and I look forward to it with great anticipation every year.

About 1990, a few of us die-hard collectors came up with an idea to meet at a hotel the Friday night before the show. This gave us all a chance to see what everybody else had before the show started. It also made dealing between us easier, because once the show began, you were stuck at your table. Many great agates have traded hands on the Friday night before the show.

Aside from the other dealers, the best opportunity to see and buy trophy lakers is from people walking into the show. It's ridiculous, really. While everybody is busy selling agates and other wares, I always have one eye on the lookout for somebody walking in with a big one. I also keep an eye on the other tailgaters. If I see one of the "boys" leave his table, it can be only one of two possibilities: they're either heading for the bathroom, or they've spotted someone with an agate. You can usually tell by how fast they're walking-they usually move faster if it's an agate.

It is not, however, always the first one who talks to the person with the rock who gets it. Many times people are there just to show off their most recent find. Of those who are looking to sell, the smart ones will talk to more than one tailgater to see who will pay the most. There have been many memorable Moose Lake shows and

Co-founders of Moose Lake Agate Days, Floyd Clark and Tom Olson at the September 1971 show. The next year they held the first "Agate stampede" on Main street.

many memorable agates. I've seen many good ones walk in, and I have definitely landed my share of nice trophies. I don't, however, get all the good agates at Moose Lake that I'd like to. In 1998, I ran into one of the toughest negotiators I ever met. A young boy, about eight or nine years old, walked up to my table carrying a three-to four-pounder. My eyes locked in on the rock, and I could instantly see it was a super. I asked the young fellow if I could look at it. I slowly turned the nearly round stone in my hands, carefully examining it. The agate was mostly white with red banding. It was a dandy all right, but it needed to be cleaned and oiled. This one would be a lot of fun to clean up, if only I could buy it.

I gave the agate back to him and offered him enough money to buy a brand new bicycle. I was sure that offer would do the trick. He smiled and looked up at his father. His dad said, "It's your agate, do what you want." He then looked back at me and said, "No thanks." He told me that he found it that spring, and it was the biggest one he'd ever found. I was thinking that it was probably the biggest

One of the tough negotiators that I couldn't crack at the 1998 Moose Lake Agate Days show. He got me so flustered, I forgot to get his name and number. If you see this photo of yourself and want to give me another chance, give me a call.

agate he'd find the rest of his life. Sensing his hesitation, I made a second offer. "How about enough money for two bikes?" He laughed and said, "No, I think I want to keep it." I grudgingly realized that I had met my match and asked if I could take a picture. Then he walked off to the next table cradling his treasure. I kick myself for not getting his name. If I ever see that kid again, I'll make him an offer he can't refuse. Who would turn down enough money for three bikes? As intense as it sometimes gets, every year we all end up with at least one nice prize for the display case.

In 2000, over three thousand people attended the thirty-first annual show. Each year it gets a little bigger and more fun. The agate stampede on the main street on

Saturday afternoon is another unique part of Moose Lake Agate Days that makes this show special. The frenzy for agates during the stampede is sometimes so intense that adults have been known to push children aside in their frantic search. Although I didn't push the little kid that hard. Besides the blast from the cannon going off, I know the stampede is under way by the temporary sparseness of the crowd in the tailgating area. For anyone looking to buy, sell, trade, or just see good Lake Superior agates, Moose Lake Agate Days is the place to be.

Janet coaches as two-year-old Grant learns the art of agate picking at the 1992 Moose Lake Agate Days stampede.

At the 1987 Moose Lake show, I met a person who recruited me on a mission that would result in the realization of a dream. That person was a Lutheran minister with an unrelenting passion for Lake Superior agates. His idea was to pursue a state park with agates and the geologic history of Minnesota as its focus. The fanatical minister's name is Phil Gotsch.

I'll have to admit that the first time I heard him lay out his plan, I thought he had spent a little too much time in the gravel pit. The idea was interesting, but I didn't think anyone would take it seriously. After hearing more details, I realized a couple of things. First, it was obvious that he knew something about working with politicians. We would need to do a lot of back-scratching of legislators to make this thing happen. Second, Phil had more than enough agate fire inside to keep such a cause moving ahead. I was the first recruit in Phil's army, and after fourteen years of service, it looks like I will be in it for life.

Phil deserves all the credit. He knew exactly what had to be done. We solicited support from state representatives and senators. We also contacted members of rock-hound clubs, the chamber of commerce in Moose Lake, and people in the Parks Department of the Department of Natural Resources (DNR). Bill Morrisey, the director of the Parks Department, was an early supporter. I was quite impressed, watching the seeds of communication bear fruit. The first victory, in 1991, was when the state published the favorable results of a feasibility study. The next major event was in 1997, when the state legislature appropriated $30,000 for the design of a building. With the state actually giving us a meaningful amount of money, we knew we were almost there.

In the 2000 legislature session we had the right people in place, pushing the right buttons. Representatives Mary Murphy and Bill Hilty, along with State Senator Becky Laurey, were the key people who helped. In June, the phone rang and it was that familiar voice I'd spoken with dozens of times. "Scott, the state gave us one million dollars for the park!" I couldn't believe it. After all this time, that crazy idea had finally come true. A few weeks later, we had a barbeque to celebrate. Even though we felt a great deal of pride for seeing a dream come true, the real winners are the people who will visit the park. Generations of agate lovers will be able to see, learn, and enjoy the Lake Superior agate story. The agates themselves will also benefit. There will be a permanent home for specimen donations and a place for collectors like me to share our treasures. Rotating displays of private collections will ensure that there will always be different specimens to entice people to come back. We plan to invite everyone who helped with the project to a ground breaking celebration, at Moose Lake Agate Days, before construction begins in the fall of 2002.

Reverend Phil Gotsch (right) and I pose with our materials of education and persuasion about Lake Superior agates in February 1994. We were lobbying legislators at the Minnesota State Capital for the proposed Agate/Geological Interpretive Center.

As we toasted ourselves for a job well done, we reminisced about the long and hard, but successful, journey. I don't know what made me buy into this agate-crazy minister's idea, but I'm sure glad I did.

Sharing some new specimens with my agate mentor George Flaim at the 1999 Moose Lake show.

The Second Edition

By the summer of 1993 I thought that the agate book had run its course. In almost seven years, we had sold the more than seven thousand books that we had printed. We made all of our money back and then some. As you can probably guess, every dollar of profit went into buying new agates for our growing collection. Most important, I had been able to heal from the trauma of losing Dad. Overall, my life had definitely gotten back on track.

There were many times when I would sit back and think about how lucky I was. I had a challenging job working in the geologic field that I love. I had an intelligent and beautiful wife who tolerates the excesses of my unusual hobby. I also had my wonderful three-year-old son, Grant. The void my father left will always be there, but I was finally starting to like myself again. The agate book played a huge role in getting things turned around. As much fun as the whole experience had been, it seemed that it was time to let the agate book sail off into the sunset. Little did I know, The Lake Superior Agate wasn't dead yet.

One day I received a call from a customer in the Upper Peninsula of Michigan who wanted to order more agate books. I thanked him for his past business and told him they were all gone. I also told him that I wasn't going to print any more. To my surprise, he offered to buy the rights to the book. Why I never thought about that before, I don't know, but it was a great idea. I told him I'd think about it and call him back. After considering the idea for a short time, I quickly realized that I didn't know where to start. I was flattered that he was interested, but I had no idea what the rights to the book might be worth. The only thing I could think of was to pull out the Yellow Pages and look under publishing.

I don't remember why I picked Burgess to call first, other than their name was near the front of the alphabet. When I called and asked if I could talk to someone about selling a book, I was transferred to a fellow named Jon. His was very friendly and showed immediate interest as I explained the situation. The more I told him, the more interested he seemed. After a brief conversation, he said he wanted to get together to talk more. A couple of days later, I walked into the Burgess Publishing office and sat down across the desk from director of publishing Jon Earl. Jon was warm and friendly with a positive, can-do attitude that quickly put me at ease. We hit it off right away, and little did I realize at the time, we would eventually become good friends.

My main objective when I first arrived was to learn all I could about what my book might be worth. By the time I left, Jon said that Burgess would be interested in purchasing the rights. He also said that they would be interested in doing a second edi-

Jon Earl holds the second edition of the *Lake Superior Agate,* released in the spring of 1994.

tion. When he asked me if I could write more about agates and add more photographs, I laughed. I could tell agate stories until I lost my voice. I also had enough new agates to photograph that would easily fill another book. When I walked out of there, I was so pumped up I nearly floated home.

The next time we got together, I signed a contract to sell the rights to the book to Burgess and begin work on the second edition. Even though I could probably have done something with my friend in Michigan, it made more sense to do a deal closer to home where I could keep an eye on things. Over the next six months, I spent a lot of time at their offices. Another benefit of working with Burgess was that they paid all the expenses. I was afforded a modest budget to help pay for camera rental and film development. This time, instead of hiring someone else to take the photos, I was determined to do them all myself. I was excited about the challenge, and I would find out how much fun photography is.

On two different weekends I rented a 120 mm color-transparency camera with lights. The first weekend was cold and snowy, in mid-January. I hit the road, and my first stop was at the Braun family farmhouse in Altoona, Wisconsin. They were wonderful hosts, and I spent four hours listening to their stories about Michipocoten Island and photographing their incredible collection of agates. As big and beautiful as they were, I had this strange feeling about these agates. They were clearly lakers, but because they were never touched by the glaciers, something was missing. Or wasn't missing. These agates were all completely intact. They had to be cut to see the beauty. As nice as they were, they just didn't compare to the natural exposure of color and banding of glacial agates. To find a beautifully exposed natural laker is difficult. The rarity makes them special. Regardless, the Michipocoten agates are certainly unique and wonderful in their own right.

From there I headed north to Duluth to shoot more agates at George Flaim's house. One memorable agate we shot was Terry Roses's Peanut Butter and Jelly Agate. Many people would eventually say that it was their favorite agate in the second edition.

Every time I see that rock I think back to Moose Lake Agate Days a year or two before I photographed it. A fellow came by my table trying to sell a nice-shaped, but otherwise unimpressive two-pound agate. The stone was a yellowish-orange colored nodule with no obvious banding exposed. He said he wanted $200 for it, and I thought he was nuts. No one else wanted it either, so he took it home, put it into a saw, and polished it. The next year he came around with the agate again. I couldn't believe it was the same one and this time, it wasn't for sale. All of us who passed on it were kicking ourselves. That agate turned out to be an awesome specimen. As that fellow found out, sometimes it's better to be lucky than good.

The second photo shooting weekend was at my house. I invited several collectors over, and as luck would have it, we had a heck of a snowstorm. No matter, the agate diehards would not be denied. John Harris drove over from Eau Claire, Wisconsin, just to shoot one picture of his marble collection. While I snapped away at individual specimens on one side of the basement, I glanced over at Bill Steffes working feverishly setting up another photo. He spent over two hours carefully positioning his eye agates for a group shot. His persistence paid off; the eye agate photo is still one of my all-time favorite agate images.

My absolute favorite photograph however, is the fortification agate group shot. I probably spent as much time as Bill did setting up his agates. Each one had to be strategically placed with the face turned up just right. Janet just watched and shook her head at this classic display of my compulsive agate behavior. Once the agates were ready on the floor, I placed the camera on the pool table with the lens pointing straight down. I knew right away when I saw the transparency that this image would be the cover photo for the new book. In fact, I liked it so much that I had posters and a five-hundred-piece puzzle made. Seven years later, they're still selling.

In addition to taking portraits of agates, I've taken a lot of photographs of structures inside agates, under the microscope. It's absolutely incredible how beautiful and complex agates are under magnification. There is no doubt in my mind that the secret to agate formation will eventually be solved when the microstructures within agates are finally understood. I've tried to speculate on the origin of the structures within and how they formed. I will certainly continue to do so, but the strongest motivation for me to look so closely at agates is really quite simple. At every level, Lake Superior agates inspire wonder at their beauty. Many people have written letters or called saying how much they enjoyed the pictures *inside* agates.

When the second edition sold out in 1994, Jon said, "Let's do one more." Once again I added more text and photographs and published the third edition of The Lake Superior Agate. By the end of 2000, we had sold over twelve thousand copies of the three editions and it continues to sell. Burgess has let me do whatever I wanted with the book and been supportive since the day I walked in the door. We certainly haven't gotten rich with the agate book, but we sure have had a lot of fun. I will always be grateful to Burgess for that.

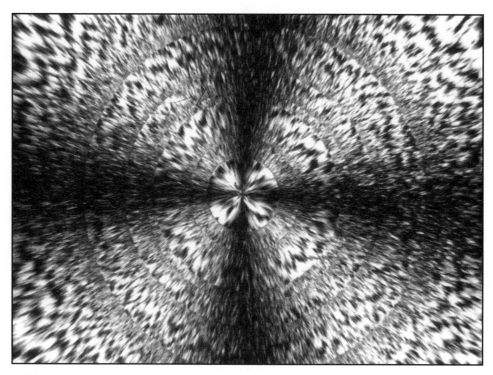

Banded tube structure of a Lake Superior agate in thin section (approximately twenty microns thick), under cross-polarized light (40x). The radiating chalcedony fibers are always aligned perpendicular to the banding plane. This rounded form of chalcedony in agate is called spherulites. Many believe these structures are the key to agate genesis and dictate internal structures during formation.

A scanning electron microscopic image (100x) of a fractured piece of banded agate. The thinner layers are coarser chalcedony crystals that form the white bands in a small candy-stripper.

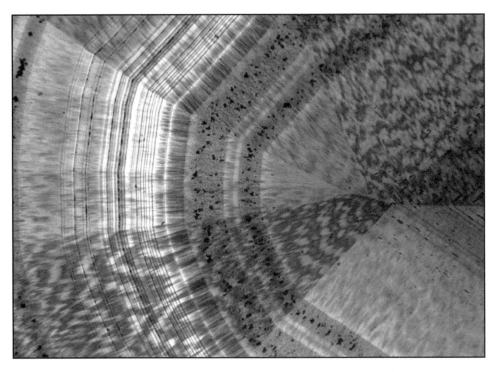

The sharp turns that banding makes in some agates are called chevron patterns. This paint agate thin section captures several such patterns under plane polarized light (40X).

White shadow banding seems to disappear as it pinches down at the "fill hole" of this agate (17X). The exact mechanism that produces this feature in agates is a hotly debated subject.

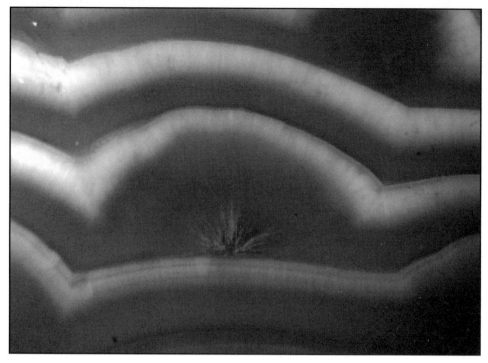

A radiating plume of iron-oxide deflects the white bands on top. It appears as though the banding developed one-at-a-time starting at the bottom (25X).

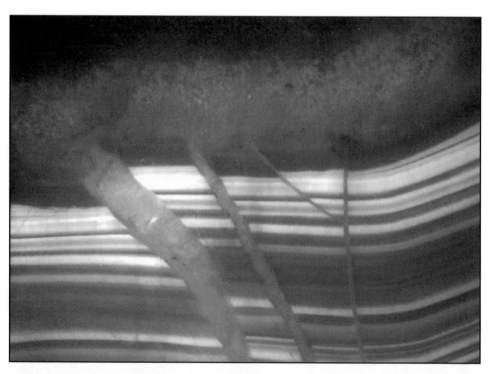

"Healed" fractures in this ruin agate do not extend into the crystalline quartz center of the agate. This feature clearly indicates multiple events of silica deposition during formation (15x).

The Work of
Glaciers On Agates

Most people who know me realize my preference for naturally eroded, rough glacial agates. I've always felt that there is nothing more beautiful than what nature can create over time. What makes Lake Superior agates different from all the other agates found around the world is their long and interesting past. Lake Superior agates are certainly the oldest; their formation dates back over a billion years. They are also unique in that they contain a relatively high amount of iron pigment within the silica host. Basically, Lake Superior agates formed within volcanic gas pockets of lava flows, the same as many other agate types. What sets lakers apart from all other agates is their glacial history.

Beginning about two million years ago, thick lobes of glacial ice flowed into North America, including Minnesota. The ice originated from a huge, three-mile-thick dome centered over what is now Hudson Bay in Canada. The glaciers were up to a mile thick in Minnesota and carried millions of tons of rock, including agates plucked from bedrock they passed over. The ice sheet that did all the work is called the Superior lobe. It flowed over the birthplace of agates, which is now occupied by a large body of fresh water called Lake Superior. As the glacier moved forward, the agates were taken on an often violent journey. To truly appreciate how agates were transported and eventually deposited over such a vast area, you need to understand how glacial ice works.

I was intrigued by the glacial processes that produced Minnesota's hilly terrain and numerous lakes while studying geology in college. Even more important to me was to understand the glacial processes that worked on agates. Not only did understanding glaciers help in appreciating the beauty of agates, but that knowledge was extremely useful in finding them. Fortunately for me, I was able to learn from one of the world's experts, Charles Matsch. Charlie was not only a brilliant glacial geologist, but an excellent teacher. He made learning interesting and fun, but demanded a lot from his students.

By the spring of 1979, I'd spent most of my college career playing sports, dating girls, and partying. I went to UMD on a football scholarship, and for the first two years I basically majored in eligibility. I worked just hard enough to get the grades I needed to keep playing football. I didn't know what I wanted for a major until I met Charlie.

I had signed up for an elective class called Introduction to Geology, and Charlie was the instructor. At the end of the quarter, I had done a pretty good job in the class. One of Charlie's requirements was to have a personal meeting with each student. When it was my turn, he surprised me. He said, "You have a talent for geol-

Sharing a laugh with Charlie Matsch at a 1997 reunion of UMD geology graduates in Duluth, Minnesota.

ogy, but I don't know if you have what it takes to make it." I thought to myself, "Oh, really?" I looked at him and said, "What else have you got?" I have to admit that I liked Charlie and respected him. He had a great sense of humor, and I knew he was trying the old negative sell to challenge me. He said, "I'm teaching geomorphology next quarter, but I don't know if you can handle it?" I laughed and said, "Let's give it a try."

Geomorphology is the study of land forms. A good chunk of the time spent in class was on the work of glaciers on the landscape. It was fascinating to learn how complex ice could be. As Charlie lectured on how glaciers move and the deposits they leave behind, I kept imagining agates in the mix. Glaciers are incredibly dynamic. The intense weight and pressure of the ice rips and tears at bedrock to create massive quantities of boulders, gravel, and sand. When the ice eventually melts, an incredible amount of water flows from on top of and beneath the ice. The ice continually melts and numerous streams wash out sand, gravel, and clay. As the ice repeatedly advances and melts back, the material is reworked over and over again. The margins of a glacier are surprisingly active. It became easy to imagine how Lake Superior agates ended up the way they did. Once the banding was exposed, the iron within began to oxidize, producing the beautiful colors.

When the ice melted away for the last time, about ten thousand years ago, over fourteen thousand lakes were left in Minnesota alone. Along the rocky beaches of the large lakes, prolonged wave action put the finishing touches on many lucky lakers. These are the special, baby-bottom smooth gemstones we call water-washed agates.

As I gained a better understanding of the rough road our agates had taken, I had a whole new appreciation for them. When the class was over, I had earned an A. This time, I asked Charlie for a personal meeting. I told him how much I enjoyed his class and thanked him for putting a spark in me. For the first time in my academic career, I was excited about something besides football. Charlie asked if I would be interested in pursuing a degree in geology. "Yeah, I would like to," I said, "but under one condition-I want you to be my advisor." Charlie looked surprised then smiled and said "OK."

The next three years were challenging, but with Charlie's skillfull guidance, I received my geology degree in May 1982. I had taken every glacial geology class that the university offered. Each class helped me to understand not only everything related to glaciers, but also Lake Superior agates. This is probably the reason I overwhelmingly prefer rough, natural specimens. It started off this way, and entering the new millennium, I still love lakers the old-fashioned way-natural.

Over the last several years, however, I have broadened my collecting focus and developed an appreciation for polished agates. As I say this, I still cringe a little. There have been many wonderful lakers that have been butchered by inexperienced or indifferent collectors. I've seen everything from polished or cut agates that should have been left alone, to fantastic large agates that were smashed with a hammer.

There are two problems with cutting and polishing Lake Superior agates. The first is that most of the color on the surface is secondary. Most lakers are dominantly gray and white internally. It is the years of glacial erosion and weathering that have produced the brilliant colors. If

Very small-scale, normal faulting of sand and gravel deposited by melting glaciers over twelve thousand years ago. Janet poses for scale on a warm summer day in 1985.

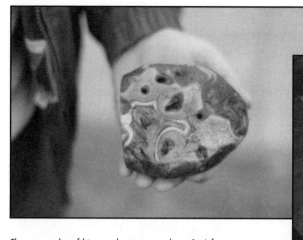

Three examples of big, rough agate tragedies. **A.** A fantastic 3.50-pound specimen that had one end cut off through the large beautiful face. **B.** A spectacular laker that weighed almost nine pounds *after* it was cut into three pieces. This agate would have made the top ten list if it had been left alone.

C. This agate which we call Crying Shame, was probably around three pounds before it was thrown against a train trestle over sixty years ago. The pieces that could be were glued back together.

the oxidation color or "staining" is polished off, the colors usually fade and sometimes disappear. Many lakers have what I like to call "true" color, where the iron-oxide pigment is so thick and prevalent that even when polished the color holds. These are the exception, but they do occur. The second problem is cracks and internal fractures. The very thing that makes lakers beautiful and unique is the reason internal fractures are so prevalent. The periodic, violent impacts and severe freeze-thaw exposure over thousands of years have left our gemstones beautiful, but internally flawed. When a rough agate is polished, the fractures are highlighted. The tough part is that the fractures in a rough stone are virtually impossible to see. What may look like a flawless stone, even after close examination, will end up with at least one visible fracture, although there are rare exceptions.

Careful study of selected stones finds that some agates would be better if they are polished. I think I'm beginning to understand this, and I have cut and polished some pretty nice ones. I've waited as long as six years before deciding to do something. It definitely pays to be patient; once you cut or polish a stone, you can't go back. So far I've had pretty good luck.

The Night of
The Lake Superior Agates I & II

Two special events have taken place since my first agate book came out that specifically honored Lake Superior agates. The idea for the first event came up while my picking partner, Mike Carlson, and I were out collecting agates in the summer of 1986. The first edition of this book was almost completed, and we were wondering how it would be received. Would it stimulate interest or sputter out of the blocks? We talked about ways to promote the book and to figure out a way to see as many agates as we could. Eventually, we came up with the idea of having a special program about Lake Superior agates, different from what people were used to. Normally, a club program included a guest speaker who brought along a few specimens for people to see. Mike and I were thinking bigger, much bigger. We wanted to host the Super Bowl of Lake Superior agates.

We decided to invite all the people we knew to come and display their best agates. We each knew several people with great collections and invited all of them to come. Many of these people lived out of state, and we weren't sure how many would attend. We were both pretty confident of a good turnout because the lure of agates is pretty strong. We reasoned that any true laker collector couldn't turn down an invitation to see the grandest collection of agates ever assembled for one night only. Our reasoning turned out to be right on the money.

Mike has been an active member of the Minnesota Mineral Club for many years and asked if the club would help. The club members were highly enthusiastic and offered to sponsor the event. The first thing we did was to find a large enough space for the many expected displays. As program director, Mike was able to secure a gymnasium at the Logan Park Community Center in north Minneapolis. The club members helped send out flyers to other mineral clubs and rock shops.

It was my job to solicit the collectors whom I knew to bring their best agates to display. The job turned out to be much easier than I thought it would be. Most were happy to come. I only had to twist a couple of arms. We received commitments from people all over Minnesota, Wisconsin, and Iowa, as well as collectors from Nebraska, Missouri, and Michigan.

We also contacted local media, both newspaper and television. Our persistence got us a guest plug for the event on the Good Company show on KMSP-TV. Mike even wrote a letter inviting then governor Rudy Perpich to the event. Although he was unable to attend, the governor sent a warmly worded letter in support of our Night of the Agates.

The day of the show was hot and sunny. By late morning, people began arriving at the Wolter house. We had advertised the event as display only, so I invited

Friends and family members each hold a Lake Superior agate while on the *Good Company* show in May 1987. We were there to promote the first Night of the Lake Superior Agates.

the collectors who wanted to buy, sell, or trade agates to come to a preshow agate pow-wow.

Several of the most rabid collectors showed up from around the upper Midwest. Janet and I laid out a barbeque buffet lunch that everyone seemed to enjoy. After lunch, the agate dealing began in earnest. Before we knew it, there were hundreds of agates laid out all over the front yard. They looked especially beautiful in the natural sunlight. Guys would move from pile to pile throwing trade and purchase offers. What a riot we had!

By 4:30 P.M. it was time to pack up and head down to the show. We formed a caravan into Minneapolis. Once we arrived, everyone began setting up their displays. There were cases full of agates lining three walls of the gymnasium. My head was spinning around looking at everyone else's agates while I tried to set up my own collection. Soon the doors were opened, and people began to filter in. The gym filled quickly with people anxious to see the agates. I was also inundated by people with questions and kind words about my new agate book. I was fortunate to have Janet there to help with selling the books while I was blabbing away. The night flew by, and soon it was time for the formal program. Mike was the emcee and did the introductions. He thanked the Mineral Club members and other volunteers who worked so hard to make the show a big success. The night concluded with my slide program, and I was able to personally thank everyone for their support of the book. By the feedback and turnout we had, it seemed that the book helped pump new life into the Lake Superior agate hobby. Many people told me the book helped ignite their interest to become new collectors. I also heard from people who said their old agate passion had been rekindled. What a thrill to have touched so many people in a positive way. It truly was a night to remember.

For the next several years, Mike and I often reminisced about the fun and success of the first agate night. Many people suggested we have an annual display show. As much fun as it was, it was a lot of work, too much to do every year. Besides, the fact that it was a special, one-time event is what brought out so many collectors. In 1996, Mike and I were out once again, picking agates. As we trudged along through one of our favorite pits, we talked about the Night of the Agates. The following spring would be the ten-year anniversary. We agreed that it might be time to do it again.

STATE OF MINNESOTA

OFFICE OF THE GOVERNOR

ST. PAUL 55155

RUDY PERPICH
GOVERNOR

May 9, 1987

Night of the Superior Agates
c/o Michael Carlson
4501 Abbott Avenue South
Minneapolis, Minnesota 55410

Dear Friends:

I am delighted to have this opportunity to send greetings to
everyone attending the Night of the Superior Agates
gathering this evening in Minneapolis.

Your enthusiasm for collecting and sharing some of the
state's and nation's best stones is to be commended.
Rockhounding is one of the most invigorating and yet
relaxing of sports, and I wish I had more time for it
myself.

In the case of the Lake Superior Agate, I can see why you
find it so fascinating. It is a beautiful stone which can be
used in many ways, and it is indeed a perfect representation
of the State of Minnesota.

My best wishes to all of you for an enjoyable Night of the
Superior Agates, and for much future success with your
rockhounding!

Sincerely,

RUDY PERPICH
Governor

AN EQUAL OPPORTUNITY EMPLOYER

The letter then governor Rudy Perpich sent acknowledging our special agate night.

The date for Night of the Agates II was set as close to the original anniversary as possible, and we went through the whole ritual again. This time we solicited the help of our good friend, the Reverend Phil Gotsch. Phil's passion for Lake Superior agates and his dedication to a worthwhile cause is unquestioned. When the Minnesota

A terrific collection of big lakers courtesy of Brian Costigan at the Night of the Lake Superior Agates II in May 1997.

Agate/Geological Interpretive Center has its opening ceremonies, Phil can take great pride. This project was his brainchild from the beginning and its lifeblood for all these years. He is truly amazing. It didn't take long for him to come through again. Phil was able to secure St. Philip's Lutheran Church in Fridley, Minnesota, for the site of the show. The fellowship hall was huge, with room for collectors' displays along the perimeter and four hundred chairs in the middle.

Over five hundred people attended the show, but it seemed more like five thousand. As I gazed over the enthusiastic crowd, I realized something very encouraging. For many years the crowds at gem and mineral shows had been experiencing a disturbing trend. The people who attended were mostly older, and their numbers were in steady decline. The reasons were understandable-primarily, the fast-paced lifestyles of the younger generations and the decreasing number of good specimen-collecting sites. This downward trend in rock hounding had been going on for about three decades. When I looked at this group, I noticed a good percentage of the people were younger. There were many more people at this event than at the first one. It seems the upward trend in agate collecting we saw ten years ago has continued.

Even as our world seems to go faster and faster, there must be something inside us that periodically needs to slow things down. People are perhaps rediscovering rock collecting as a way to escape the madness and get back in touch with the natural world. For someone who has felt, at times, like I've been swimming against the current in my agate pursuits, I couldn't help feeling that maybe the tide was changing. The whole agate night went so well that it felt like I was cruising with the current.

As on the first agate night, I wrapped up the show with a slide program on agates, revised especially for the occasion. I always enjoy sharing agate stories with those eager to hear them, but this night was especially fun. Before starting, I had a chance to thank everyone again for their continued support of the agate book and making the effort to attend the show. I noticed Michael sitting in the front row and he gave me a thumbs-up. We smiled as if reading each other's mind. We knew there was going to be a third night of the agates. The only question was if we should wait ten years for the next one.

The richly colored wraparound face on this 1.32-pounder inspired the name, "Sandwich Agate."

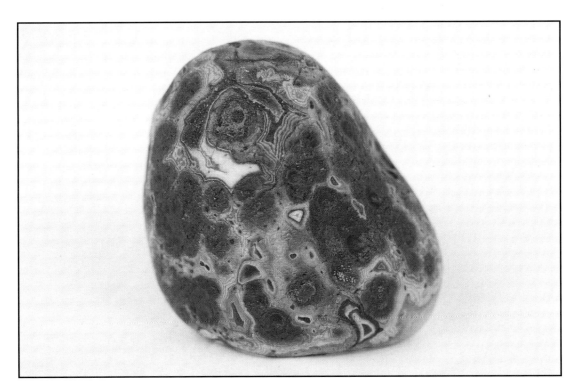

A smooth, busy and attractive "husk" on a laker is always good. This 1.72-pounder was found in a farm field near Fort Ripley, Minnesota in 1992.

Doug Eggert was hauling gravel in a pit when he spotted this 0.93-pound beauty from his truck in 1995.

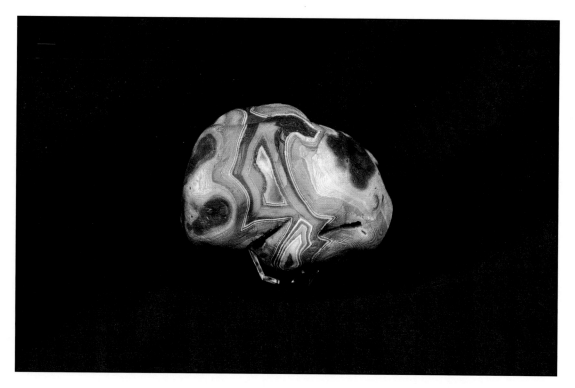

One of the best lakers (1.00 pound) Jerry Barnett found over the many years he picked agates.

I bought this 1.34-pound Bruce Peddle skong at the 1995 Austin Gem and Mineral Show.

I picked this 1.81-pound beauty up from Gary Egge at the 1999 Moose Lake show. Gary found it in a gravel pit near Red Wing, Minnesota.

The swirling pattern on this 1.94-pound beauty looks like lava pouring off a minature volcano.
Craig Litchey found this agate in a gravel pit near Two Harbors, Minnesota, in the summer of 1997.

I found this 1.97-pound paint agate in June 1988 on top of a glacial esker that had been cleared of trees and brush for mining gravel.
After an overnight downpour, I decided to go picking instead of attending a rock swap. I made the right choice that day.

Carrie Ohme showed up at my table at the 2000 Moose Lake Agate Days show after Charlie Matsch suggested she show it to me. Carrie found the agate in a gravel pit near Twig, Minnesota, in May of the same year. After getting over the initial shock, we were able to come to terms on this awesome 2.53-pound jewel.

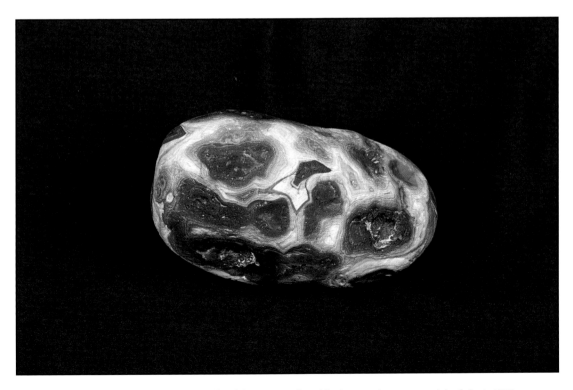

Terri Whipple was six years old when she found this 2.79-pounder, while she was picking agates with her father in 1959.

If there is such a thing as a perfect agate, this one is it. This 1.70-pound specimen was found somewhere in central Minnesota over thirty years ago and has beautiful size, shape, color, and banding quality.

I first saw this 1.72-pound agate walk into the 1995 Agate Days show and instantly fell for it. Five years later I was able to make a trade for it.

The color in this 2.22-pound agate is some of the richest I've ever seen.

This 2.22-pound agate was found by Mrs. Keuning in a Two Harbors, Minnesota, gravel pit in the 1960s.

Perhaps the prettiest paint-stone I've ever seen.
This 3.45-pound beauty was literally seconds away from being cut in half when Bob Reineck acquired it in 1988.

I knew right away when I bought it that George Flaim had owned this 3.59-pound beauty in the past. When I showed it to him, he laughed and told about finding the agate along the shore of Island Lake, Minnesota, about 1970. I remember seeing this agate for sale at the J & M rock shop, but I passed it over. For years I regretted not buying it. Sixteen years later I got another chance and grabbed it!

This 3.85-pounder was found near Pease, Minnesota sometime before 1980.

This 4.38-pound, flesh and green colored paint-stone has some of the most unusual colors you will ever see.

Greg Clark excitedly called me the day after he found this fantastic 3.66-pound paint-stone in November 1998. He found it in an area where I've been picking for almost twenty years. This agate looks like a big brother to the sky-blue paint I found ten years earlier.

Bruce Peddle skonged this 4.42-pound super from the farmer who found it in his field near Sobieski, Minnesota, in April 2000.

Cindy Kuepers found this 4.68-pound beauty while picking rocks in a farm field in 1978.

Another huge (4.86 pounds) treasure, found on a farm near Milaca, Minnesota, in 1994.

Tim Fitzgerald found this 7.48-pounder in October of 1997 while building a foundation for a home in Byron, Minnesota.

In September 1996, John Jensen found this 7.78-pound beast while fishing in the Crown River near Finland, Minnesota.

While doing landscape work in the yard of a Stillwater, Minnesota, home in 1994, John Putzier spotted this behemoth 7.87-pound agate. He offered the homeowner $10 for the rock, and was refused. The homeowner said, "It means nothing to me, you can have it!"

Bobbye Flategraff was nine years old in 1970 when she found this 8.51-pound monster in a field on the family farm near Pine River, Minnesota, after falling off her bike.

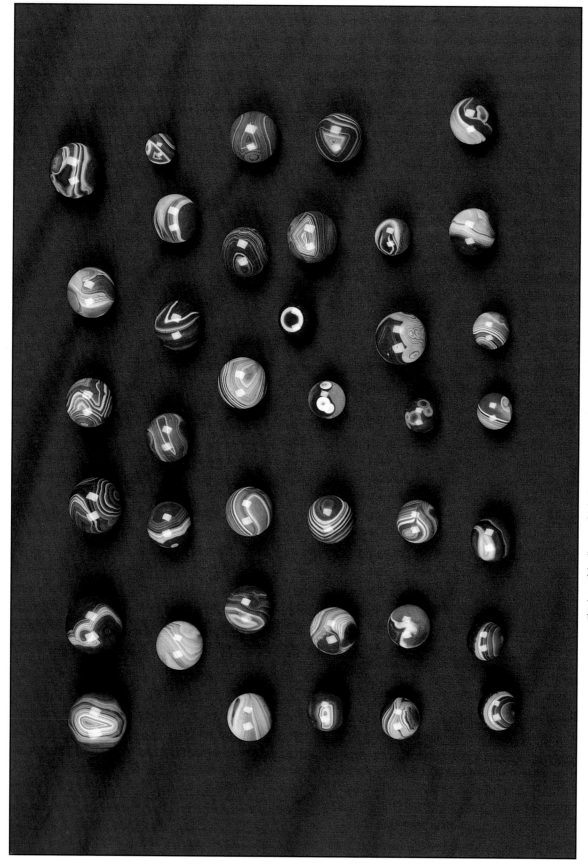

This beautiful collection of Lake Superior agate marbles were made by John and Dave Harris.

Can you match these rough agates with the marbles they were made into in the previous photo? The answers are on page 172.

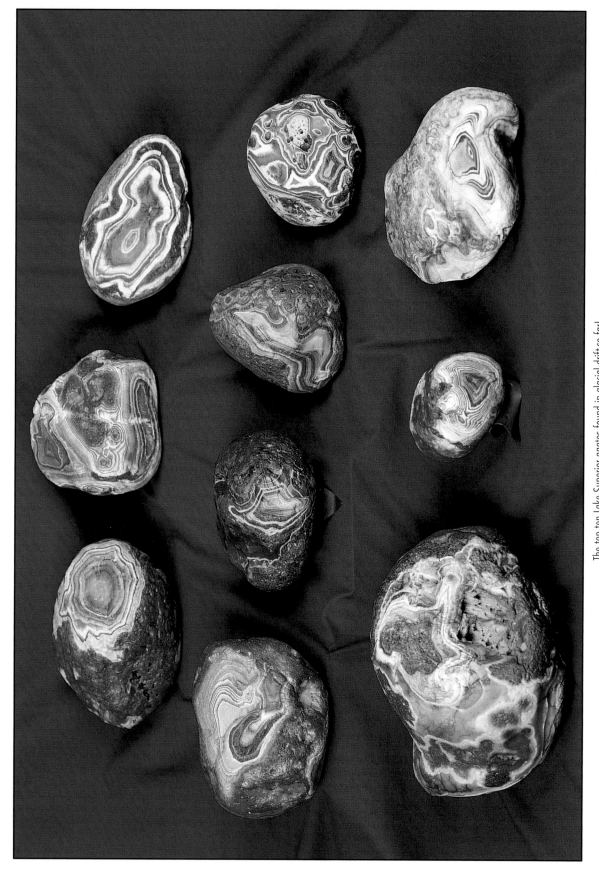

The top ten Lake Superior agates found in glacial drift-so far!

(Left to right, top row: Ham, Minnehaha Falls, Six-Pound Red and White, middle row: Strawberry Point, Berghuis, Engagement, Jingle Bells, bottom row: Counsell, Bread Loaf, Moore).

Dredging for
Agate Gifts

I'll be the first to admit that I've been extremely fortunate with all the adventures I've had pursuing Lake Superior agates. I've met many wonderful people and had tremendous luck in acquiring some of the finest specimens ever collected. Recently, however, I enjoyed one of the most fun agate experiences ever.

On a warm, May morning in 1998, I was working away at my desk when the phone rang. I quickly recognized the distinct British accent of one of my customers. Jonathan Wilmshurst is the president of Aggregate Industries, a large company that operates several aggregate quarries and ready mix plants in the Twin Cities area.

I assumed he wanted to talk to me about a problem with concrete or aggregate. As it turned out, he needed help with something else. He relayed how the company was hosting a convention and was expecting thirty to forty guests. For each guest, they wanted to give a gift that was Minnesota related. Even better would be something that would also tie in with their aggregate business. He was obviously thinking about Lake Superior agates and had come to the right place.

After discussing a few ideas, we settled on giving each person a 1½" to 2" agate encased inside a plastic cube with the company logo. He said that he could get the cubes made, and facetiously asked if I could provide the agates. I smiled and said, "Yes, I think so." He asked me if any of the agates I had were found in any of their gravel pits. I said, "Sure, but I couldn't tell you which ones." He got quiet for a second, but I could hear the wheels turning in his head. "You know, Scott, it would be nice if we could say that the agates had all come from our gravel pits." Before I could even think of it, he asked me how long it would take to find that many agates, and asked if I knew about the dredge in Maple Grove. I knew about the dredge all right, and I could feel my pulse rate increase just thinking about it.

A smile curled up on my face as I thought about the clam bucket scooping up fresh sand and gravel from underwater. I had seen the dredge in action, and it's an agate picker's fantasy. Not only is the gravel wet and glistening as it is pulled out, but all the rocks, including agates, come out sparkling clean.

I told Jonathan what a great idea it was and that I would be happy to help him out. He said, "We'll pay you of course!" At that point I started laughing. I said, "No way, if anything I should be paying you!" He said that I could keep the agates I found that were too big to be used for the cubes, but that he would like one bigger agate for his desk. I thought , "No problem." I jokingly said, "I don't know how long this project will take, but I'm guessing it will be a very long time."

As soon as I hung up the phone, I looked at the clock. I thought, "Why not start today?" I waited an hour or so and then called up Karen at the weigh-scale shack. Sure enough, Jonathan had called her and given the green light. I barely made it until 2:30 P.M., when my excitement took over. I had talked myself into going up there to scout out the pit. I jumped in my truck and in twenty minutes I was at the weigh-scale shack checking in. Karen was a pleasant lady who said she was a busy grandmother and didn't have time for agates. I told her that by the time this project was over, we'd make a rock hound out of her. She informed me that the dredge was being repaired and wouldn't be ready for a week or so, but before I had a chance to get depressed, she said they were still mining gravel with the drag line. I would soon find out the difference between a drag line and a dredge.

Before heading over to the mining area, I thought I'd "warm up" my picking skills by stopping at the processed 1 1/2" stone where I found a half dozen or so small agates. When I found a freshly fractured, colorful chip of an agate that was obviously much larger, I decided I'd had enough, I wanted to look where I could find agates that had not been through the crusher. As I drove along the conveyor belt into the active pit area, I could see the expanding lake being created by the constant removal of material below the water table. It had been well over a year since I'd been in this pit, and it looked completely different. What had once been a secluded series of interconnecting bowls of gravel pits, now had a paved road running through the middle of it. The pits had been mined to the point where they had merged into one giant open-air pit. The mining had switched to the removal of gravel from underwater.

As I pulled up to the crane at the edge of the lake, I could see the freshly dumped piles of sand and gravel. A steady stream of water trickled away from the piles as the saturated raw glacial debris was left to drain. The following day the material would be loaded onto the conveyor for the half-mile trip to the plant. Before "diving in," I introduced myself to the loader operator. Warren was a pleasant fellow who promised not to drive over me while he was working. He suggested that I check in with the crane operator. I drove over near the crane and walked up to get the operator's attention. Because of the tattoo on his shoulder, I knew I wouldn't have a problem remembering his name-Scott. He knew what agates were and seemed interested in helping out any way he could. We even talked about the best way to dump each load to bring out the coarsest gravel. I knew for sure that if I was going to find agates, I could not ask for a better situation. Each time Scott dumped out a fresh load, I'd run over and scan the virgin material. I had an average of about two minutes between loads and that was just enough time to see all the rocks. After about an hour, I had found about thirty agates, the biggest was around a half pound. There were lot's of cute little ones, but nothing really good. I quickly realized that to fill the order for Jonathan, I was going to have to spend many hours at the pit. I was more than ready for the challenge.

The next evening a big storm rolled through with a heavy downpour. As I lay in bed listening to the thunder and flashes of lightning, I quickly made up my mind where I was going in the morning. When I woke up, I headed straight for the pit. The bad news was that the drag line had a mechanical problem and wasn't working.

Scott Halverson operates the dragline in 1998 while I anxiously wait for the next load.

A heaping load of wet sand and gravel is dumped. I had just enough time between loads to pick the growing pile for agates.

The good news was that there were all kinds of fresh gravel that had been moved around by Warren in the loader, the rock had been washed off, and it was prime for picking. I found several smaller agates again and eventually decided to look around on the other side of the lake, at some older gravelly areas that hadn't been worked in a while. I knew the rock had been laying out for some time, for as I approached, I could see foot-tall weeds throughout the area. Since I had scoured the recently worked area, and the dredge was down, I figured, "Why not?" I walked around the steep shore of the young lake to the area with the most gravel. I had looked only a couple of minutes when I realized that this area had not been previously picked. Lying wide open was a 1 3/4-pounder. I felt that sudden gush of adrenaline as I instinctively bent over to pick it up. The agate was mostly gray with two large white bleached areas on exposed faces. Not an "all timer," but it had good size and it was solid. My enthusiasm was suddenly jump-started as I realized this was a virgin site with perfectly clean rock. I turned toward the lake, took a couple of steps, and my eyes zoomed in on another stone. The husk had the typical pockmarked surface of an agate, only this time it was red in color. The adrenaline pushed another jolt as I picked up the 1 1/4-pounder. This one was a complete nodule with only a small half-inch-diameter red-banded face exposed. The shape was good with no major fractures or clacks. It was a very nice agate, but I knew right away that this one needed to be cut and polished. I stood there for a second relishing the moment. Finding two big agates in less than a minute does not happen often. This project was really getting fun.

I found several small agates in the older area and then strolled back to the dredge to share my finds. Scott introduced me to the two fellows who were repairing the dredge. Milan and Paul were the morning and evening dredge operators, and they said, "Wait until we get this baby going, you'll love that." Paul proceeded to give me a tour of the floating dredge. We put life jackets on and climbed up a ladder onto the conveyor belt system that led out onto a large raft. The conveyor was shut down while repairs were being made. As we walked down the catwalk, I imagined all the fresh sand and rock zipping along on the belt and grabbing a super as it went on by. Milan and Paul operated the dredge from an enclosed room that looked like a metal tree fort about fifteen feet above the water. Everything was computerized, complete with push-button hydraulics and a depth finder.

The clam bucket, with it's jaws wide open, was lowered by a steel cable into the water by a tilting crane. Dan, the plant supervisor, later informed me that the lake they were making with the dredge would eventually be up to seventy-five feet deep. When the clam bucket was pulled up with a heaping load of fresh material, water was allowed to drain for a few seconds as the crane slowly tilted and opened over a

The dredge with the clam bucket lowered sometimes up to seventy-five feet below the surface to extract material.

The clam bucket is lowered over the grizzly where the jaws open to dump the up to six-cubic-yard load.

steel grate at the top of the hopper, dumping up to six cubic yards of material. The grate had steel bars spaced six inches apart to catch the oversized boulders. Periodically, when enough large rocks accumulated, Paul engaged a steel rake called a grizzly. The rake pulled the boulders off the grate, down a chute into a crusher. The crushed boulders ended up on the main conveyor with everything else. I wouldn't even let myself think about an agate being pulled up that was big enough to get mauled by the grizzly.

The sand and gravel fell onto a series of vibrating plastic screens that sorted the material by size. The top screen let anything smaller than one and a half inches fall through. Everything larger bounced and rolled down the screen and eventually fell onto the conveyor to be stockpiled for processing. The one-and-a-half-inch screen was about seven feet wide and sixteen feet long. Right where the rocks fall off the screen onto the conveyor was a spot for me. Paul said, "You sit right there and you'll see 'em coming." You can probably guess what was going through my mind. If there's a heaven for agate pickers, this was it. Paul said the dredge would be ready the following Monday. I began counting the days.

When I drove into the pit on Monday morning, the new clam bucket was already in full swing. I jumped out of my truck, threw on a life jacket, and climbed onto the catwalk. As I approached the raft, I was awestruck by the whole operation in action. My eyes kept racing back and forth between the bucket dumping each load and the conveyor zooming by. I couldn't fight the urge to see if an agate was sneaking by on the belt. When I got to my spot at the end of the vibrating screen, the rock was bouncing by in waves. I was so excited I nearly dove right onto the

Any rock that doesn't fall through the 1½" screen came tumbling toward me perfectly clean and wet. It was a dream situation.

screen. I quickly realized the folly in that idea and slowly climbed up and found a spot that was safe. It took an hour or so before I figured out the best position to be in without getting my legs pelted with rocks or being shaken to my bones by the vibration. Eventually, I got comfortable and trained my eyes on the sea of gravel marching toward me. The only word I can use is overwhelming. My eyes were darting back and forth trying to see every rock. The rocks were wet, which was helpful, but the water also made sand stick to each one, making it harder to identify them. The rocks were coming so fast that I felt like I was missing the agates. A new load was dumped every ninety seconds. This meant I only had a few seconds to collect myself between each cavalcade of rock, and only an instant to grab any stone I thought might be an agate. It took me a few hours before I felt that I had things under relatively good control. The toughest part was that the rocks were always moving. The constant bouncing and rolling made it really tough to figure out what something was. Regardless, this was the opportunity of a lifetime, and I was going to maximize it.

The first agate I saw come tumbling down, was a three-quarter-pounder. I spotted the dark reddish-purple husk and grabbed it. When I rolled it over, I saw a nice, small, gray-banded face. Not a flashy stone at all, but it gave me confidence. If something spectacular came tumbling down, I knew now that I would see it. I found a couple smaller ones that first day, but nothing to get wild about. The next day I showed up at 7:00 A.M. and Milan had the dredge going strong. I put on the life jacket and climbed into position ready for action. After an hour or so I hadn't seen a thing. Agate pickers know that, like many things in life, you have to keep yourself mentally charged. It's easy to get discouraged when you're not finding anything. You have to keep telling yourself to be patient. When you least expect it, that's when they show up. If you are out in the field or pit somewhere, you have all the time you need. The agates aren't going anywhere. This way of picking agates was more mentally taxing. If you are not paying attention, the agates will drop out of sight, and be gone.

I spotted the first good one shortly after 8:00 A.M. I saw the banding pattern of a half pounder just before it rolled to the end of the screen. As I grabbed it and saw the red and white bands, I felt the rush. Of course, I did what I always do when I find a nice one, wish that it was bigger. I jammed it into my pocket and started looking for the next one. Four hours later, I decided to call it a day. My body and eyes had had enough vibrating machines and rocks for one day. I had found only three other insignificant agates, and I left feeling a little disappointed. As I drove away, I consoled myself, once again realizing how hard it is to find a good big one. Lake Superior agates are rare even under the best circumstances. I was spoiled a little by the two I had found the other day. It was going to take persistence and patience. If I kept that in mind, sooner or later I would be rewarded.

The first meaningful trip to the dredge pit was on the Fourth of July weekend in 1998. The previous day I'd spent a couple of hours at my spot on the screen and snagged a half a dozen or so agates. A couple were decent halfers, but nothing great. As I sat there, I occasionally glanced up at the sky to see if the forecasted showers were moving in. There were plenty of clouds but no rain. I was hoping the rain would come and wash off the twenty-foot-high piles that the conveyor was continually adding material to. Even though the larger rocks were clean and wet as they came across the screen, they accumulated silt and sand once they fell onto the conveyor. The rocks in the piles were just dirty enough to make it hard to tell what they were. Even a light rain would be enough. Later that night, as I was crawling into bed, I saw flashes of lightning from an encroaching storm. My "agate alarm clock" woke me up at 4:30 A.M. just as the downpour ended. When I told Janet I was going picking, she gave me that "you're a madman" look and said, "Good luck."

The light was just enough to see the perfectly washed rocks even though the sun wouldn't hit the horizon for a half hour or so. The first agate I found was probably the best of the day. It was a blaze red and white nodule just over a half pound. I found it at the top of the cone-shaped pile and felt rewarded for putting in the effort of climbing up the shifting pile. The next good one turned out to be over a pound and a half about ten minutes later. This one was sitting in a sandy area on piles that were moved by the loader away from the cone pile. The agate was well banded with fortification faces coming out all over. A small plug of quartz kept it from being a super but it was the biggest and best so far. I also pulled out several supers from the one-and-a-half-inch pile. When I finally went home at 10:30 A.M. I had an ice cream bucket full of agates-one of my best days.

By the end of the year, I had enough colorful beauties for the agate cubes. I also picked out two nice one-pounders and had them polished for Jonathan's desk as I had promised. Instead of putting them on his desk, he gave them to his daughters

Emily and Sophie. Jonathan later told me that the agate cubes were a big hit at the convention and that I could continue my plunder at the dredge.

After a relatively mild winter, the dredge began in earnest in early May 1999. I made my first appearance in the third week, and the guys seemed happy to see me. Warren was his cheerful self running the loader and Milan and Paul made me feel welcome after the long layoff. I spent three hours sitting at the end of the screen, and it paid off with a beautiful, solid purple, pink and white three-quarter-pounder. It was a great start.

By this time I had become pretty experienced at picking agates on the dredge. I could tell how good a load was just by the sound it made as it was dropped into the hopper. If the bucket load was sandy with relatively little rock, it was quiet and flowed out onto the screen like quicksand. I'd often have to lean back to keep from getting hit with the soupy sand spray. This kind of load was disappointing because what rock was there I could hardly see. On the other hand, if the load sounded like a thousand people banging on the hopper with hammers, I knew good gravel was coming. Sometimes the load was nothing but larger-sized rock that made a distinct, loud rattling noise as thousands of clean, wet rocks came rolling down. These were the loads that made my adrenaline soar because I almost always found an agate. Only an agate die-hard can understand this rush. It was agate heaven!

I had renewed vigor to pick this year, for a couple of reasons. First, I learned that Aggregate Industries had signed a lease to mine gravel using the dredge for about two more years. After that, the Maple Grove operation would be shut down for good. Second, in the last few years it had become increasingly more difficult to find or purchase good agates. Many of the good big ones collected years ago have been shaken out of the closet over the last dozen or so years and are in various collections. Last, I thought about the relatively little time I'd spent picking the two years before this opportunity came along. Increased work and family pressures had taken up most of my time. I probably needed the time away from picking to recharge my batteries. Well, the dredge had recharged my agate batteries and they were ready to go. I was definitely going to take full advantage of this wonderful opportunity.

The morning after I found the nice agate, I visited with Milan for a few minutes. He asked me if it would be easier for me if they welded a platform behind the wall at the end of the screen. I said, "You bet." To stand over the screen without all the vibration would make a world of difference. He pulled out his tape measure and said he'd see what he could do. When I showed up two days later, I couldn't believe my eyes. The steel platform was already done. Paul had finished it the previous day. How spoiled can I get? I decided I had to do something nice for him. Paul had told me that he used to have a grill on the tower platform, but someone had stolen it. Later that day, I took Grant and Amanda to Target and bought a small grill.

The next day was Saturday, and Paul would be running the dredge till 4:00 P.M. I decided to pick the whole day and showed up at 9:00 A.M. Paul had a puzzled look on his face as I walked down the catwalk with that box in my hand. He climbed from his perch and met me at the platform. I said "Thanks for the picking perch," and gave

Amanda and Grant inspect a great pile of agates I found on the July 4th weekend of 1998.

him the grill. His face lit up and he immediately started planning a cookout. Eventually he said, "Let's get this thing going and find a good one." Not ten minutes later, I saw a red and white bull's eye face marching down the screen. It was a super red-and-white nodule, the best agate I'd found to date. Over the next six hours I found twenty-five agates, including three more nice ones. By the time Paul shut the machine down for the day, I had a sunburned back of the neck, but a nice bucket of beauties. I must have been rewarded for returning a good deed.

After three years of enjoying this wonderful opportunity, the dredge was retired for good. I spent hundreds of hours picking there and found dozens of beautiful agates. In all the millions of rocks I looked at on the dredge, I only found a handful over two pounds in size. Of those, I would not consider any of them an all-timer. It was further proof of how tough the truly good, big ones are to find, even under the most ideal conditions.

Two roughly one-pound agates I found within ten minutes on the dredge.

My pal Paul Schroeder holds a nice 1.67-pounder we found on the dredge in the summer of 2000.

Copper
Harbor

For sixteen years I've been looking for a good reason to go scuba diving again. I think about Dad and what happened every day. As rough as it was, I never said to myself that my scuba diving days were over. It's just that the thrill of being underwater just wasn't there anymore. The phantom agate dive at the Grant cabin was my only dive since Australia. Deep down inside I knew I'd get back in the water again someday; I just needed time and the right motivation. The spark that lit my desire was a big, burly guy named Jake Anderson.

Jake and his wife run a dive shop in Copper Harbor, Michigan. We first met them in August 1999 while on a family trip to the Upper Peninsula. For our two nights in Copper Harbor we stayed in a motor home at the Fort Wilkins campground. On the first night, I went into the liquor store in town to buy some beer and noticed that there were banded rocks on the shelves. After a closer look, I saw that they were agates. Most of them were pieces broken off of much larger stones, and they certainly got my attention. I asked, "Where did you get these?" The man said, "Jake found them while diving in the big lake." "Who's Jake?" I asked. He said, "He runs the dive shop down the street. You can't miss it." I thought, "Now we're cooking."

I bought the beer and headed down the street to find the dive shop. Even though I knew it would be closed, curiosity was driving me now. A minute later I was pressing my face against the shop's glass windows trying to make out the shapes inside a glass display case. The sun had just set, and I needed a flashlight to see inside. I paused for a second and thought, "Wouldn't that be great if a patrolman arrested me because he thought I was trying to break in?" All I wanted was to see the rocks inside the case, and there was no way I was going to wait until the next morning.

I put the flashlight against the glass and peered in again. Sure enough, the case was filled with big agates. I couldn't tell how good they were, but they definitely had size. I scanned around the case and spotted something else that instantly brought a smile to my face. In the middle of the case, encircled by agates, was the most recent edition of my agate book. This Jake guy and I were going to get along.

The family and I strolled into the shop at 9:00 A.M. sharp the next morning. The man behind the counter was tall, burly, and looked to be in his midfifties. His bare chest was protruding from a brightly colored Hawaiian shirt that had only the bottom two buttons fastened. He reminded me of my Canadian grandfather who spent his life logging trees and living large. He did everything with gusto and never worried about the other guy's opinion.

He looked at me and said, "What can I do for you, Bud?" I introduced myself and my family, and a smile came to his face. He said, "You're the guy who wrote that book." He introduced us to his wife, Laura, and we quickly plunged into agate talk. Jake and I hit it off instantly. I asked him to show me his gems. Each time he handed me one from the case he told how he found it. They were all found underwater while scuba diving, some in gravel reefs and others chipped out of bedrock. I was fascinated. One in particular grabbed my eye. It was about three pounds or so and was a beautiful, orangish-red paint-stone with an amazing amount of white banding. Jake told me how he and a friend named George had used four air tanks to chip the agate out of the bedrock. He said, "That's only a chip out of it, the rest is at home." My eyes suddenly widened. The rest of it is at home? I knew right away that if I was going to try to buy an agate, this is the one I wanted.

Big Jake Anderson welcomes us aboard his boat. We spent over nine hours in Lake Superior finding agates on a perfect August 2000 day.

For years I have wondered about the birthplace of Lake Superior agates. My curiosity was especially piqued after meeting the Braun family and seeing their amazing Michipicoten Island agates. I told myself that someday I would have to visit that island and see these monster lakers still sitting in the rock they formed in. It turns out that Lake Superior agates are found in the host rock here, also. As Jake and I talked about his agate adventures while scuba diving, I couldn't help thinking that this was the place, and the person, to get me back into the water again.

Eventually I inquired about the big paint, and we reached a tentative deal. Laura watched the shop while Jake jumped into his truck and led us along the lake to his home. Along the way he pulled over next to a telephone pole to show the kids some deep scratches in the pole about six feet off the ground. Jan and I smiled, watching Grant's and Amanda's eyes widen as Jake told how a black bear had stood on its hind legs and sharpened its claws on the pole. Inside their beautiful home overlooking the lake, Jake put the five other pieces of the agate into my hands. He explained how the agates usually break up when they're chipped out of the bedrock. I was easily able to fit the pieces together into what turned out to be a nodule over ten pounds in size. What was so amazing about it was that the husk was completely intact. It even had some small pieces of the host basalt rock still attached. Normally, I would be distraught over a fantastic laker like this that was broken so badly. But it didn't bother me that much. The fractures where it broke had been there long before they had removed it. If the glacier had plucked it out on the journey, the pieces surely would have been spread out over perhaps as many states. All the pieces were here, I just needed to glue them back together.

Jake asked me if I would be interested in diving for lakers with him sometime. I was ready to go that very second, but there wasn't any time on this trip. I told him I would be back. For the next ten months, I kept thinking about what was in that lake and when I would get the chance to find out. One thing I would not have to worry about when diving for lakers was footprints at the bottom of Lake Superior.

In early July the following summer, I called Jake and said I was coming up. On the eight-hour drive from the Twin Cities, I had a lot of time to think. Dad would have loved to do this dive with me. He was always ready and raring to go on a new adventure. Even though he wouldn't be there in the flesh, he'd be there in my heart.

I made it into Copper Harbor by 7:00 P.M. Laura and Jake filled me up with burgers off the grill, and after dinner we watched the sun set over the lake as we planned our dives for the next day. Jake said we'd stay in the harbor and look at some agates in the bedrock, and then the following day we'd cruise out on the big lake to his favorite gravel reef. It was 11:00 P.M. before we knew it and time to turn in. I was pretty fired up, so it took me a while to fall asleep. The next thing I remember was hearing the patter of little legs running down the stairs as their pet beagle jumped onto the bed and licked my face. I groggily wandered upstairs where Laura had coffee and breakfast waiting. "Jake's down at the shop and said to come down when you're ready."

When I pulled up to the shop, Jake was loading the scuba gear into his truck. I jumped out and started helping. Another truck pulled up, and a big blond fellow in his mid thirties got out and introduced himself. He was Jake's underwater agate-picking partner, George Twardzik. My first thought when I saw George's broad shoulders was how good he'd look in a Lumberjack uniform. It turns out he is a local football legend in Copper Harbor. We had two things of common interest, football and agates. After loading the gear, we drove down to the public dock and loaded everything again, this time into Jake's twenty-five-foot long boat.

We shoved off and headed out a mile and a half to the other side of the harbor. George dropped the anchor in ten feet of water about seventy-five yards from shore.

Underwater agate fanatic George Twardzik in September 2000, shortly before shoving off on a successful trip.

Jake turned to us and said, "Get your suits on, boys, we're getting wet!" I can honestly say that I really wasn't that apprehensive about getting back in the water after so long a time. I was too excited about finding agates to get the jitters. Besides, with two experienced divers going with me, it was a perfect situation. George jumped in first and swam down to check the anchor. He waited a few feet below the surface for me to jump in. Jake helped me put on the weight belt and air tank. He quickly refreshed me on all the equipment and emergency procedures. I climbed onto the rear platform and gave Jake the thumbs-up. I put the regulator in my mouth, took a breath, and stepped out and splashed into the water.

I could feel the cool lake water penetrate the wet suit and instantly warm up as it touched my skin. After only a few seconds, that old familiar feeling returned. I was comfortable and excited at the same time, just like the old days. I turned around to find George and gave him the OK sign. Just then a mass of tiny air bubbles appeared as Jake plunged into the water. He quickly checked on both George and me and then led us off into the abyss. The water was beautifully clear and perfectly lit by a bright, sunny sky. The bottom started off a little weedy, but quickly turned rocky as we swam. Jake surfaced to check his location, and within a minute he found what he was looking for. I followed behind him, scanning the bottom, suddenly a bright white and pink circle appeared on the bottom. George and Jake were on either side as I swam up to what must have been twenty-to thirty-pound agate in the bedrock. I put my mask within a foot of the monster. Although the circular nodule was mostly quartz, there was beautiful gray and white banding around the outer edge.

As I gazed at the giant, I knew it was not going back with us. It was securely embedded within its basaltic host rock. Even though it was huge, it was not good enough in quality to be worth the effort to remove it. I motioned Jake to the surface and suggested that we leave it where it was.

George and Jake shadowed me the whole dive. They went out of their way to make sure I had a good experience, and I most certainly did. After an hour and a half of scouring the bottom, we returned to the boat. Jake said this dive was a good

136

start and that things would only get better. It didn't take long for me to find out that he wasn't kidding.

Later that same day, Jake and I took off in his fourteen-foot fishing boat to the mouth of the harbor. Basalt bedrock was protruding from the waves, and as we approached, I noticed the wet, dark gray rock was peppered with orange spots. After a closer look I realized the "spots" were dime-to silver dollar-sized paint agates. I smiled and hustled to get my gear on. Jake anchored the boat, and we rolled over the side into the shallow water. At a depth of less than five feet, the only reason we wore tanks at all was for convenience. We had brought rock hammers and a slide chisel and went to work freeing agates from the host rock. The agates were everywhere but getting them out was tough. First, swinging a hammer underwater was like watching a movie in slow motion. Holding yourself steady and getting a good whack on the chisel was hard. Second, unless there was a preexisting fracture to follow, the rock was much too hard to knock loose. Third, whenever we did chip a decent agate out, it

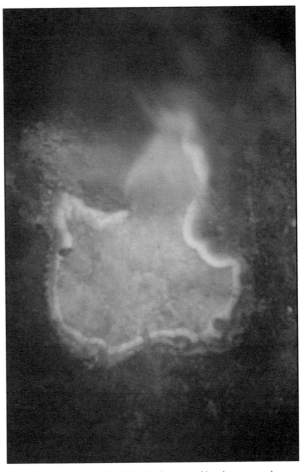

The first big agate I saw in the bedrock underwater. Although it was mostly quartz, it still was an impressive sight and had to weigh at least twenty to thirty pounds.

almost always broke into several pieces. This primitive method of agate extraction got old real quick. I couldn't handle watching those banded beauties fall apart in front of my eyes. After a couple of hours, we returned to the dock with a few nice specimens of agates still in the basalt matrix.

Later that night as we sipped a cold beer, I had a new appreciation for just how many agates there were still embedded in the host rock. I could more easily understand where all those small chips came from that we find littered in the gravel pits. Imagine how tough the glaciers were on those fragile little guys.

Bright and early the next day, the three of us headed out on the big lake. Jake had loaded six tanks onto the boat, enough for each of us to have three hours of agate-searching bottom time. Our destination was an underwater gravel bar that George and Jake had picked only once the previous year.

As Jake slowed the boat about a quarter mile offshore, he pointed to a spot straight off the bow. I looked out on the lake and could see small swells breaking over what had to be very shallow water. The gravel bar was just below the surface, beckoning us to check it out. We anchored in fifteen feet of water and jumped in.

As the tiny air bubbles from my plunge into the water cleared, I could see the visibility in the water was at least twenty-five feet. When I looked down at the bottom, all I could see was beautifully rounded, softball-sized gravel. I descended and noticed a mucky, green weed growing on the rocks that made identifying them a little more difficult. I brushed my hand over the muck, and it easily wiped off. I decided to head into shallower water where wave action kept the muck from forming, leaving the gravel clean and pristine.

At a depth of between three to five feet, the rock was perfect for searching for agates. The gravel ranged from pea-to fist-size with every rock vivid and bright with color. Within minutes I found a golf ball-sized orange and white paint-stone. This agate, as well as the others I found, looked exactly like the agates we find in the gravel pits back home. The difference was that nearly all the agates we found here were paint-stones, and every one of them was perfectly water-washed. After an hour and a half, I was down to five hundred pounds of air and headed back to the boat. Inside my bag I had a couple dozen, mostly smaller agates. The biggest was a very nice half-pounder.

George surfaced a couple minutes later and couldn't wait to show me a good quality, orange and white agate that was about a pound and a half in size. My competitive juices began to flow and for fun I decided to challenge him. "Hey George, I bet you a six-pack of beer I'll find a bigger agate than you on the next dive." He smiled, and laughed, and said, "You're on." Eventually, Jake showed up, and we quickly ate sandwiches, chips, and pop to recharge our batteries for the next dive. Within a couple of minutes the second set of tanks were on our backs and we went in again.

While swimming along the bottom, I thought about my strategy to win the bet from George. I had to figure out how to beat the big one he already had. There was only one way to do it. I had to look at the muck-covered, bigger rocks in the deeper water. As I began my search, I realized that I was being followed. I turned around, expecting to see George or Jake, but I was surprised to see that I was being tailed by three beautiful, foot-long whitefish. Each time I brushed the muck away from the rocks, the fish would swoop in and devour the nutrient-rich weed.

About halfway through the dive, I noticed a rock that even through the weed had a slight orangish glow. When I wiped it off, I noticed a small banded face. It was an agate, and it was big. At first glance, it looked like it was five to ten pounds. I knew that everything underwater looks 25 percent larger, but, as usual, my excitement made the agate look bigger than it was. It eventually came in at three pounds, still a big agate. Even though it contained a fair amount of crystalline quartz, it was a nice shape and beautifully water-washed. Once I had the agate safely tucked inside my rock bag, I felt confident I would give George a run for his money.

I spent the last half hour of air savoring this rare opportunity. To pick agates in a virgin gravel deposit on the bottom of Lake Superior was a rare and special treat. It turned out my big quartz ball was enough to win the competition. George said, "I'll even the score the next time you come up." It wouldn't be long before he got his chance. Four weeks later I brought the whole family up to Copper Harbor for another go-round.

For this trip, we rented Jake and Laura's cabin next to the dive shop for the weekend. As we pulled the Explorer into town, I noticed a strong west wind roaring off the lake. After settling into the cabin, we all took a walk down to the dock in the harbor. We looked out at the peninsula and heard what sounded like a freight train roaring through the woods. In the distance we could see white caps on the lake, pounding the shore outside the harbor. I knew for sure that we were not going diving on the big lake this day.

As disappointed as I was that we could not go back out to the underwater gravel bar, we still had fun diving in the harbor. George, Jake, and I spent over two hours finding golf ball-sized bangers that afternoon. We had a great time, but my heart yearned to get back out on the open water. By nightfall the wind had died down considerably. The forecast was for a high pressure system, which meant the next day should be calm and sunny. The wind would have to die down for us to make it out to our gravel bar. We went to sleep that night hoping our last day on this trip would be memorable.

Once again, Jake was already loading tanks into the truck when I groggily peered out the window. The sun was just peeking over the trees to the east, and the sky was clear. The best part was that the roar of the wind through the trees we heard the day before was gone. After quickly getting dressed, I walked over to the shop to help out. As I walked up, Jake said, "Well, buddy, the lake is perfect. We're going to have a great day." For this trip, Jake had filled nine tanks, three for each of us. That meant we had enough air for almost five hours of underwater agate picking. Needless to say, I was pumped!

Janet and the kids rolled out of bed to help us load up. After a couple of minutes, a familiar truck pulled up. Out jumped George in his trademark Hawaiian shorts. He was ready to go, too! Grant helped us load the gear onto the boat then wished us luck as we shoved off. I had convinced the guys that we should go prospecting to see if we could find a different area that might have agates. After a forty-five-minute ride from Copper Harbor, the depth finder started to indicate shallow water. We were several hundred yards offshore when we started to see huge boulders on the bottom. Within a couple of minutes we were in about fifteen feet of water. Jake pulled the throttle back and yelled to me, "Do you want me to drag you?" I thought, "What a great idea!"

I already had my wetsuit on, so I grabbed a mask, snorkel, and fins and jumped in. George tossed me rope as Jake slowly started the boat forward. I put my face down into the water and began scanning the bottom. Conditions could not have been more perfect-sunny sky, about eighty degrees, and excellent visibility. I could easily see the smooth bedrock and loose boulders pass below.

George was on the bow looking out for large boulders and shallow spots. At one point, I heard the motor disengage and the boat quickly stop. I looked up and saw George pointing at something in the water. We were in about ten feet of water, and George called to me, "Scott, go check out that white rock down there." I swam over to the spot and took a breath. As I started down, I saw it. On my first attempt, I couldn't get a good grip on it. I resurfaced for another breath and tried again. This time, I grabbed the twenty-pound or so block-shaped rock with both hands and started up. It was heavy, but I made it. I handed the stone to George who set it down on the rear landing. It was a white quartz vein with part of the host rock still attached on one end. Between the quartz and basalt was a 2" wide, banded layer of orange-colored agate. We knew this had to be a good spot. It was time to drop anchor.

I climbed back into the boat, and we all put our gear on. We were still a couple hundred yards offshore in ten to twelve feet of water. Our plan was for each of us to scout around for gravel bars and areas with agate in the bedrock. After piling rocks onto the anchor, we set off to find banded treasure. Not fifty yards from the boat, I spotted my first agate in the bedrock. Like most of the agates I saw in the harbor, it was an orange paint-stone. I peered in closer at the roughly one-pound stone and could see a familiar green color in parts of the banding. The green was malachite, a weathered copper mineral common in this area of the Upper Peninsula. When I looked around, I could see agates of all sizes peppered in the smooth bedrock. I continued on, exhilarated, wondering if I was the first human to see this magnificent sight.

As I slowly made my way toward shore, I saw hundreds of agates embedded in the bottom. Several agates were easily over ten pounds in size, including one that was over three feet long. I nearly choked on my regulator a couple of times as I swam over many fantastic specimens. Any one of them would be the crown jewel of my picking career had I found them the old-fashioned way. In a way, it was like being tortured. Many of these spectacular specimens beckoned to me, but they were in jail and I didn't have the key.

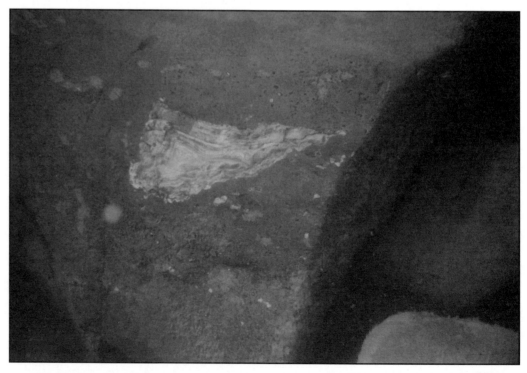

An eight-inch-long laker, still embedded in a large basalt boulder in about ten feet of water.

I did find one neat specimen early in my search while swimming over intermittent pockets of gravel, which were scattered in low spots on the bottom. In one of these gravel areas, I noticed a familiar orange glow. I swam down and picked up a softball-sized basalt cobble containing a one-pound agate. It had a complete fortification face with three pronounced filled fractures, running parallel through the face. It was a champion ruin agate with fractures that continued into the basalt.

Eventually I worked my way to the shore. When I was just a few yards off the beach, I switched to snorkeling to conserve my air. For a while, I frolicked on my belly, finding marble-sized agates as the breaking waves tossed me around. After a little over two hours of prospecting, I began to make my way back. Not far from the boat, I came upon Jake and George, who had stumbled upon a big agate they thought they could get out. The bedrock protrusion they were chipping on was within a few feet of the surface. I checked out the situation and concluded that they were going to be there a while. Once on board, I removed my tank and weight belt. Instead of grabbing another full tank of air, I decided to try snorkeling instead. I jumped back in the water, and after checking on the boys, I headed off again.

Over the next four and a half hours I must have swum three or four miles and seen thousands of agates. Whenever I saw an agate loose on the bottom, I stuffed it inside my wetsuit. On my way back this time, I found Jake and George pounding away trying to free a different big agate. When I tapped on Jake's shoulder, he surfaced and took his regulator out. He said, "Go check out a beauty I found. Just head for that log, you can't miss it," and pointed toward the beach. I told him I'd meet him on the boat and swam off. About fifty yards away and roughly the same distance from shore, I began to see a pocket of agates in the rock. Suddenly I saw it. No doubt about it, this was the one he was talking about. I spread my hand over the banded face to get a feel for how big it was. It had to be at least five pounds in size. The agate had a perfectly banded, oval pattern with orange, red, purple, and white colors. The center had a golf ball-sized pocket of white quartz with orange floating bands down to a spot. Best of all, it had shadow in the banding. It looked like a giant eye staring right back at me. I knew instantly why they didn't try to get this one out. The host rock was so dense and solid that it would have come out in a thousand pieces had they tried. It wasn't going anywhere. It turned out that the agate they were working on fell apart, too.

Once we were all back on board, it was now early afternoon, and we pondered what to do. Should we head back to Copper Harbor or burn up the three remaining tanks of air? Within ten minutes we were back in the water on the same gravel bar we had such great luck on last trip. I knew this would be my last dive of the year, so I savored every minute. The sun was inching toward the horizon, and the gravel took on a deep, rich glow. My mind began to wander as I picked up each small agate. I had learned so many new things about our wonderful lakers. The first thing was that the billion-year-old lava flows had given birth to an amazing number of these jewels. It floored me how many agates I could see exposed at the surface. Imagine how many there are at depth in the rock. The second thing was now I had to rethink the processes of how Lake Superior agates end up the way they do when we find them in glacial deposits. I had always pictured agates being freed from the host rock virtually intact. What I saw on the bottom changed all that. Many features that I had assumed to be produced solely by glaciers were present in agates still locked in the rock.

The glacial agates we often find that clearly had been part of a much larger agate were probably broken apart the moment they were freed by the ice. I also saw many agates in the rock exhibiting peeled texture, bleaching, and oxidation colors. The beautiful, big agate Jake found had one of the most desirable traits an agate can have, a perfect water-washed face. The more I thought about it, the more I realized that I really shouldn't be that surprised. These agates have kept me in wonder for over twenty years, and it shows no sign of stopping. Just when I think I'm starting to figure things out, they throw me another curveball.

I was just beginning to make my way back to the boat when I heard a banging noise. I surfaced and saw Jake on the rear landing, calling me in. As usual I was the last one out of the water. It was now almost 6:00 P.M., and long past the time we said we'd be back. I had spent nearly nine hours in the water and still didn't want to leave. We each had a sack full of agates and great stories to tell. On the trip back, I laughed while George and Jake went through each agate and threw back the ones that didn't make the quality cut. I sipped a cold beer and watched the magnificent view of the peninsula go by, and a smile came. I realized that the spark in me to scuba dive had returned. Instead of feeling sad about my father, I thought about how much fun I was having with these two agate diehards. It took a couple of new friends with the agate fire and my old friend "Mr. Agate" to get me back in the water for good. You can be sure that next year Jake, George and I will do it all over again.

Barron of Beef

Many people wonder why I always scramble with excitement whenever the phone rings at home or at work. It's very simple-there could be a fantastic agate adventure on the other end of the line. Such was the case when I picked up the phone at my office in late February 2000. I recognized the deep, gravelly voice as my buddy Jake from Michigan's Upper Peninsula.

He said, "I've got a big agate for you!" That cascading shiver of excitement roared through me as my mind kicked into agate mode. I didn't need to hear the details; if Jake had a big agate, it had to be good. I started firing questions at him, and to my surprise, this agate had a story like other.

Jake finds all of his agates while diving either on, or in, the bottom of Lake Superior. I assumed that was where this one came from. I was surprised when he told me it did not come out of the lake. He said that he was working with a crew near Eagle Harbor, clearing out a swampy area to make a lake. Condominiums were going to be built around the man-made lake. The development they were working on was affectionately called Fake Lake Estates by the locals.

After they cleared away the brush, they scooped out the muck with a backhoe. He said they removed six feet of clay and mud, the last foot comprised of sand, before they hit bedrock. The backhoe bucket scraped the rock at the bottom of the hole and nicked something. Jake said he looked down and saw a small reddish chip in the rock. He said, "Look at this one boys, it's an agate." The other guys on the crew said, "That's not an agate." Jake, however, knew what he was looking at.

He jumped in his car and drove home to get a hand sledge and chisel. He came back and chipped out the nodule from the relatively soft, partially weathered basalt host rock. He said he had just weighed it at the grocery store; it was 13 3/4 pounds! He asked me if I was interested in buying it. Trying to keep a calm voice I said, "Sure." He and Laura were leaving for Florida in another week, and he said he needed a little extra money to take a diver's training course. I said, "I'd love to help out. Put it in a box and send it down."

I thanked him for thinking of me, and when I hung the phone up, I got up and did a little dance around my office. Even though he said you could only see a little banding where it was chipped, I had a good feeling about this one. Besides, at almost fourteen pounds the size alone was impressive. If it had any quality at all it would be a super. Now, I had to sit and wait.

On a Monday afternoon, four days after talking with Jake, I returned to my office after lunch, and there was a box sitting on my desk. The return address was Eagle Harbor. That adrenaline rush came on again. I could feel a smile form as I slowly sat down in my chair. I had to calm myself so I didn't rip the box open in two seconds. I had to remind myself to slow down and enjoy it. Big monsters don't show up every day, and I should savor this rare moment of wonder and anticipation. I gently picked up the box, and I could feel the weight. I know it must be hard for most people to understand, but these are the agate moments I live for.

I zipped a razor knife across the top of the box and opened it up. Jake had wrapped the agate in rubber carpet backing, and I slowly peeled it back. My eyes widened as the beast unfolded before me. It was a brute, all right, and virtually intact. As I rolled the rock in my hands, I was amazed at how different this agate looked. It was mostly pinkish red in color with intermittent patches of greenish gray. The green colors were secondary minerals from the decomposing basalt matrix. Certainly some of the green was malachite from oxidizing native copper, so rich in that region. I scanned the chipped area Jake had mentioned and could easily see fine, pink banding. I brought the agate into the lab and put it under the microscope. The chip was the only area on the agate with clues as to what was on the inside. As I peered through the scope examining the fine features, I came to the conclusion that it was a huge paint-stone. The agate had beautiful, deep, rich color and easily visible fortification banding. The only question was, how much banding was there?

The whole time I was studying the stone, I had a somewhat awkward feeling. I was used to seeing Lake Superior agates that had been glaciated. Nearly every agate I have ever seen always has something showing and, usually, a lot of banding showing. This agate was big, had almost nothing showing. It was odd, but a rare treat to have a laker this big that came right out of the lava flow completely intact. Amazing.

I sat back down at my desk, cradling the giant. I spent time examining the undisturbed husk. The nodule had several sharp edges that glacial transport would surely have worn down. I even noticed a cast in the agate of what looked like swirls of ropy texture from inside the vesicle. The agate even had a nice shape. It looked a lot like a slightly lopsided birthday cake. I knew for certain-this agate needed to be cut.

I had told a couple of agate friends that I was getting a big one in the mail, and they both wanted a call the minute it arrived. I laughed when I told Janet about our powwow that day. She said we were acting like it was the birth of a baby. Well, for an agate die hard, it was.

Within fifteen minutes of my call, Bob Reineck and Paul Hisdahl were sitting in my office. I closed the door and we passed the rock around. It's great fun to get a new agate, but it's even more fun to share it with people who can really appreciate it. I also wanted to get the opinion of people knowledgeable about agates on what they thought I should do with it. Both Bob and Paul agreed that it had to be cut. We weren't, however, in total agreement as to where to cut it. Paul and I felt it would be best to cut an end off, leaving most of the rock intact. Bob had a different idea. He's a guy who likes to go for the gusto, and he said, "Let's butterfly it, cut it right in half." As tempting as the idea was, I'm not the gambler Bob is.

Besides, what if the agate was a quartz ball inside? Making the home-run cut was too risky. I wonder if he would be that brave if it was **his** rock?

The three of us chatted a while and eventually decided to set up a time to cut it. I started thinking about what a momentous agate occasion this was and thought it would be fun to invite some others. We set the time for 11:00 A.M. the next morning. After Bob and Paul left, I made a few calls. I invited a few more people I thought would enjoy a quick agate get-together.   Not only would it be a lot of fun, but soliciting more opinions seemed like a good idea.

The first one I called was Mike Carlson. Mike is one of my picking buddies, and he has been cutting and polishing agates for a long time. It turned out he was off from work that day, and he said he'd be there. Bill Steffes is an avid laker collector and does a fair amount of lapidary work, including Lake Superior agate marbles. Although a busy insurance executive, he was ready and raring to go, too. The last friend who was able to make it was Steve Nyquist. We tease Steve about being a big-shot attorney with the biggest legal firm in the Twin Cities-which he is. But whenever I call him and the subject of agates comes up, his voice gets low and everything else takes a back seat. "How big is the agate? You're going to cut it? What time? I'll be there!"

On the drive home I kept looking over at the behemoth agate next to me wondering what would happen the next day. Would it be an all-timer or a quartz ball? Impossible to say, but I had a good feeling that we were doing the right thing.

The first to show up were, who else, Bob and Paul. They waltzed into my office and said, "Let's go back to the lab and wait for the others." We drove two blocks to the building where the rock saw was, and Mike was there waiting. Everybody knew each other and had brought along at least one new agate to show off. It was a warm, sunny day, and we had a spontaneous, mini-agate powwow. Bill and Steve were running late, so we all agreed to get the show on the road.

I brought my video camera along and asked each guy to say a few words before putting the monster into the saw. Just as the camera started rolling, our boy Steve strolled into the hopelessly dusty lab in a new business suit. He looked way too sharp to be hanging around with this motley crew, but he's one of us. I put the agate in his hands and said, "Give us your prediction." Steve closed his eyes and gently rubbed the agate. After a few seconds, he opened his eyes and said, "It's going to be good."

Each participant's thoughts were recorded, and it was now show time. I lifted up the top of the saw and put the agate in. We had reached a consensus to cut the end off to see how it looked. If need be, we could always take another slice. We gave Paul the honor of pushing the on button and heard the twenty-four-inch blade kick in. We knew it would take a half hour or so to cut, so we all hopped into Mike's van to get some lunch.

The drive-through at McDonald's wasn't busy and we were back in just a few minutes. While we were munching Big Macs and fries, Bill pulled in and joined the party. Everyone who could come was now there. We were not able to get Bill's expert opinion beforehand, but at least he was there for the unveiling. After twenty-five minutes or so, it was time.

The six of us crowded around the saw, and Bob fired up the video camera. I slowly lifted the lid of the saw as Bob zoomed in on the blade. As I pulled the carriage back, the rock came into view. The agate was solid with no quartz. I let out

The Baron of Beef gang. Left to right, Bob Reineck, Paul Hisdahl, myself, Steve Nyquist, and Mike Carlson in March 2000.

a sigh of relief and peered in for a closer look. The banding was rather subtle but a beautiful pinkish-red color. We could even see green color within some of the bands. At the center of the roughly five-inch-diameter face was a quarter-sized pink and white pattern that begged to be opened up. The other notable thing was that the big agate had a lot of very fine fractures, no doubt from expansion and contraction over thousands of years of freezing and thawing near the surface.

We took the agate outside to the sunlight where the color really popped. It wasn't the all-timer I had hoped for with fat red and white banding, but it was still very nice. We all agreed it needed another slice. Since everybody had left their jobs to come over, they couldn't hang around for the second cut except for Paul. We loaded her up again. The second slice nailed it right on. That pink and white face in the center really opened up. This new face looked many times better than the first one. Even after the two cuts, the agate still weighed over eleven-and-a-half pounds.
Now that we had opened it up and were pleasantly rewarded, the next challenge was to get it polished.

Paul and I agreed that a curved face polish was the way to go. With many other types of agates, a flat lap polish is the most popular. With lakers, however, a curved "German polish" is the way to go. To me, a curved polish gives life to the stone and helps maintain the glacially rounded shape. It takes an experienced and knowledgeable craftsman to do the job right. With a stone this big it takes heavy equipment, skill, patience, and strong hands.

I asked Bob Lynch in Two Harbors to do the job. It was a daunting task, but Bob said he was up for it. I think the best way to relate the polishing experience of such a large and unique stone is to let Bob tell it himself. When I picked up the finished agate at his shop, he gave me the notes he wrote while working on it:

Bob Lynch at his shop in Two Harbors, Minnesota, holds the Baron of Beef shortly after he polished it in April 2000.

> *4-14-2000 Received agate and it appears to have many minor interior fractures. Upon rough grinding to remove cracks and to shape the agate, large pieces kept popping out, maybe 1/2" x 1/2" and up to 1/8" deep, impossible to remove cracks on coarse wheel, pieces keep pulling out. Necessary to opticon and catalyze to keep it together, took about 3 hours to cool before catalyzing.*

> *4-21-2000 2nd grind, found it necessary to use finer grinding wheel only, takes 2 to 4 times longer but cracks finish to a fine edge, ground about 1 hour. 12 pounds is a lot to hold for this long, after grinding for this long, arms ache, requires very careful grinding to avoid grooves from the wheel edges since this face is such a low crown [curve].*

> *4-25-2000 Necessary to stop and opticon again, only seals 1/16" to 1/8" below surface, after grinding small amount, chipping begins again.*

> *5-2-2000 Grind again for 45 minutes, looks better, necessary to opticon again.*

> *5-7-2000 1 hour 15 minutes steady polishing, needs a final opticon, hopefully the last, the polish is very good, some fractures still show, color is getting brighter, my shoulders ache!*

> *5-9-2000 1/2 hour polishing and it's done! The polish is fabulous, just like glass (with a few minor cracks), final weight = 11.44 lbs.*

At the end of the workday, I drove home to Chanhassen with the freshly cut behemoth in my lap. Another important duty that had yet to be done was deciding on an appropriate name. Naming agates is a great way to amuse yourself and others. It is also very useful. It makes much more sense to refer to a particular rock by name rather than saying, "You know that red and white one?" I believe that only special agates are worthy of being named, and this one certainly qualified.

I couldn't wait to show Janet and the kids what the agate looked like on the inside. Their approval was unanimous, and Jan even bestowed a special privilege to the agate. She let me leave it on the kitchen countertop next to the sink. Only important rocks are allowed to reside within her clearly defined territory.

The big agate was on the counter for only one day before it was mobile again. I always carry my newest prize around with me for a while before I carve out a permanent spot on the collection display shelf. I'll show the rock off to anyone who even looks like they might be interested. Janet has said more than once that I brag about my new agates more than I did about my kids when they were babies. That's definitely not true! But you can tell how much I like an agate by how long I haul it around with me.

The morning after, I decided to bring it to work with me. When I lifted it off the counter, with both hands, I found a note underneath. My mother-in-law Shirley had been over and noticed the stone. She deserves proper credit for the name I think fits it best. She wrote that it reminded her of a medium-rare, roast baron of beef. In Shirley's honor we named it Baron of Beef.

Anniversary Agates

If anyone out there thinks you can't find good agates anymore, think again. On a wet, rainy morning on June 4, 2000, my family and I had a memorable day. The evening before, Janet and I had celebrated our fourteenth wedding anniversary with a great dinner and a movie. We reminisced about the many fun times and good fortune we've had. We have two wonderful children that we can't believe are growing so fast. Grant is the sweetest ten-year-old boy there could possibly be, who looks like and has the calm, even temperament of his mother. My six-year-old daughter is a beautiful ball of energy who challenges us everyday. When she occasionally causes my blood pressure to rise, Janet turns to me and says, "Don't get too upset. You realize you're looking in the mirror, don't you?" All I know is that when she looks at me and says, "Hold me, Daddy," it's the greatest feeling in the world. Down the road, somebody is going to have a hard time shaking her loose from me.

The person who has been my soulmate for two decades just gets better with each day. It's amazing how much she has put up with all these years. No one else could ever match how Janet has supported my obsessive hobbies and endless involvement in sports over the years. Her unselfish love and support continues to amaze me. I will always be grateful for her standing by me for those two awful years after Dad died. I was no fun to be around, but she helped put my brain and heart back together again. When I finally came out of the fog, I realized what a find she was. Somehow I convinced her to marry me. It was the smartest and most important thing I have ever done.

Janet has also been a terrific partner in this Lake Superior agate adventure that we continue to enjoy. She shares the joy of acquiring a new treasure to add to the collection and stands ready with the water bucket when the agate flame in me burns a little too hot. Jan also knows the thrill of finding a good agate in the field. I've taken her to the pits several times over our twenty years together. Not only is she beautiful and smart, but lucky, too!

The first time I took her out was in 1980, the year we started dating. I thought it would be romantic to take a walk along the Mississippi river by the University of Minnesota campus. Not long into our stroll, I spotted several mounds of glacial gravel that had been recently dumped. The urge to look for agates kicked in, and I figured now was as good a time as any to introduce her to my secret passion. Janet was more than willing to go.

We scanned a few mounds, and in my haste I walked out in front of her trying to show off how fast I could pick out agates. After only a few steps, she called my name. I whirled around to see her holding a relatively large rock. "Is this one?" I walked back and, sure enough, she had picked up a super, half-pounder. The worst part was that "Mr. Agate" had walked right over it.

There was no way I was going to let her know how much it bugged me that she pulled one out from under my nose. Even though we had been dating only a few months, she already knew how to push my buttons. After our walk, we went to a restaurant. I had to eat my meal with her new agate propped up on the table in front of her. Throughout the meal, she had a sly grin of satisfaction on her face. The next time we go out picking I thought, I'll find the good one!

My next chance to even the score was a month or so later. We had taken a ride north on my motorcycle to the Barnum, Minnesota, area. We rode in and out of a few pits and found several small agates. Guess who found the agate of the day. We split up in a pit, and after a few minutes Jan nonchalantly wandered back to join me. After pausing a moment, she pulled her hand from behind her back and showed me another half-pound, red and white beauty. She didn't have to say anything, her smile said it all. For the second time in as many trips, Janet had out-picked "Mr. Competitive." At the time, both those rocks rated pretty high with agates I had found. As fate would have it, those agates became part of my collection anyway. On a hot, muggy Saturday, May 31, 1986, we got married.

It was almost twenty years before Janet found her next memorable agate. The previous morning I had spent three hours on the dredge looking at some awesome gravel. Paul had pulled over as close as he could get to the north bank, which was heavy with gravel. I'd found a half dozen nice half-pounders when I had to leave to coach Grant's baseball game. The rest of the day I kept wondering what gems Paul had dug up and I had missed. I vowed to return to pick the stockpiles if it rained overnight. Sure enough, a steady rapping on the roof woke me from my slumber that night. I rolled over to hear the downspout dripping with water. I smiled knowing it wasn't if we were going picking, but when.

By 8:00 A.M., both children had crawled in to cuddle with us. As much as I enjoy our family morning time, my agate furnace had kicked in, and after a few minutes it was time to get rolling. Everybody was up to the challenge and dug out their rain gear. Amanda and Grant were very excited about tromping around in the rain. Janet was a little less enthusiastic about getting soaked, but was still ready to go.

We pulled into the pit by 9:00 A.M. and parked next to the freshly washed, cone-shaped piles of gravelly sand. Janet found the first agate. It was a beautifully banded red-and-white about three ounces in size. Not one for the trophy case, but a nice start. Amanda said she wanted to pick with Daddy, so we marched off together, umbrella in hand. We strolled over to some flat areas, and Manda quickly showed her skill spotting a few agate chips. Only six years old, she didn't have the full-fledged agate fire yet. I could, however, see a candle-sized flicker of pride in her eyes each time she picked up a prize.

A steady drizzle continued, and after fifty minutes we all wandered back toward the truck. I mentioned that we should check one last stockpile before moving on.

The words were barely out of my mouth when Jan bent down and picked something up. She was three steps ahead of me at the base of the pile when she turned to face me. I looked into her wide, triumphant eyes as she held out her hand and said, "Happy anniversary, Honey." She put the rock in my hands. I saw the wet, banded face. It was a stunning red paint-stone that stopped me dead in my tracks. She had done it again. The kids huddled around, and we all marveled at Mom's find.

After making a final sweep of the pile, we all crowded into the truck to head to the next stop. As we started off, Janet passed her agate around as if to stoke the picker's flame in the rest of us. Unfortunately, the fire of one of our members had been doused with disappointment. When Jan and I turned to look in the back seat, all we could see was Grant's rain hat pulled down over his drooping head. As Janet pulled back Grant's hat, we saw tears running down his cheeks. We asked what was wrong, and he said, "I didn't find any agates." After hearing those words, I knew instantly that Dad had to do something. I told him, "Granty, the next stop, you and I are going to find a big one, OK?" Barely lifting his head, he said, "OK."

The next area was also being mined for gravel under water. This time a drag line was being used that dumped the wet gravel into a large pile. As we rumbled down into the pit next to the crane, we noticed the pile was only a fraction of its original size. Most of the material had already been hauled off for processing. No matter, we pulled up as close as we could get without getting stuck. The rain was falling steadily, and the girls decided to wait in the car. Besides, Janet had her trophy, and Manda was a soaked, muddy mess.

Grant and I marched off together with renewed optimism and focused resolve. Regardless of how we did, we were doing it together. After jumping over a few run-off streams, we approached the clean gravel pile. I prodded Grant to lead the way, and we picked up a couple of pea-sized agates. After an all-too-short scan, we turned to check out the far end of the pile that was mostly sand. As I began gesturing to Grant in the direction of the sandy pile, he suddenly stopped. Before I could look up, he excitedly pointed his arm and said, "Hey Dad, there's one." I looked over and there it was. Even from thirty feet I could see the red bands on the broad, curved face poking through the sand. We took a couple of steps closer and I said, "Don't pick it up yet, I'll go get the camera." We quickly high-fived, and I ran back to the truck.

Janet had been watching the show and was already getting her jacket on. Manda jumped out and handed me the camera. The three of us walked up next to Grant, who was jumping up and down with a huge smile, waiting to grab the rock. "Can I pick it up now, Dad;" "Not yet," I said. I wanted to get that rarest of photos, a big one before you pick it up. As I readied the camera, my beautiful daughter, who was oblivious to the situation, pointed and shouted, "Hey Daddy, there's one!" Janet and I laughed, realizing Manda had found the big agate-again!

I quickly snapped a couple of photos and turned to Grant. He looked like a thoroughbred horse ready to burst from the starting gate. "Go get it, Granty." I snapped another photo as he rolled it out, and one more with his trophy in hand. Each time I look at the agate, I can't believe how timely his find was. One thing I do know, is that proud smile on his face was priceless.

The rare photo of a big laker before it gets picked up. Grant excitedly pulls it out. The proud smile of a picker and his prize.

The Top Ten
Lake Superior Agates Of All Time

Why I didn't think to do something like this in the first book I'll never know. I was mowing the grass in 1998 when the idea came to me. With over an acre to mow, and the riding mower not running, I had three hours of push-mowing to daydream about agates.

Top ten lists are certainly nothing new, and rating the top agates has undoubtedly been discussed by collectors in casual conversations many times. I know I certainly have. Many people have asked me, "What is your favorite agate in your collection?" What I like to say is, "If the house was on fire, and I could only grab one as I was running out, it would be..." Sorry, you'll have to wait for the countdown to know which one!

With the lawnmower chomping away at the seemingly endless field of grass, I started to make out a list of favorite agates in my head. I began to think about the different aspects that I felt qualified a laker for all-time status. I thought about what other people might think is important in a truly fine specimen. I decided to seek out the opinions of other agate experts. The next day (yes, I finished the lawn, and eventually my father-in-law fixed the riding mower), I mailed ten letters to collectors I thought would enjoy this agate exercise as well as provide honest and informed insight. These individuals were picked for their knowledge and experience in the Lake Superior agate hobby.

Although each person I asked had something a little different to say, they all agreed on four specific parameters for judging: size, shape, color, and banding quality. Not surprising is that nearly all of the "crown jewels" are fortification agates with a myriad of beautiful banding patterns. The fact that color is important is also not unexpected. Lakers occur in a wide variety of colors, but it seems that the most attractive and popular color scheme, is the classic red and white.

The other two parameters were best summarized during a conversation I had with George Flaim. Of all the people I've met in the hobby, I respect George's opinion most. He said he had owned many agates with good banding quality and exposure, but there was always something wrong with them. Either the stone had an unusual shape that was distracting, or a good part of the original stone was missing. Odd-shaped agates can be interesting, but they seem to be the ones that you sell first or pass over when buying. Broken agates, whether hit by a plow in the field or fractured extensively during glacial transport, always leave you wondering where the rest of it went. He also said that you can find many super-quality, half-to one-pound lakers, both polished and in the rough. The all-timers that you never forget are the well-banded, good-shaped, colorful agates that are big. The bigger they are, the rarer they are. Size matters! Other people might disagree, but I think George is right. All my favorite agates have these qualities.

One thing that I think will make this list so much fun is that people are bound to disagree with some of the choices, maybe even argue. That's all right with me. Fifty or a hundred years from now, many new outstanding specimens will no doubt change this list. For now, the experts have made their selections, and the votes have been tabulated. In case you are wondering, yes, I made out my own list and, ultimately, had the deciding vote. That's the advantage of doing your own book! Well, here they are. We'll start with number ten and work up to number one. I hope you have as much fun reading this as I had writing it.

Gary Thompson in May of 1987, holding the "Counsell Agate." Gary displayed his wonderful collection of lakers at the first "Night of the Lake Superior Agate."

10. The Counsell Agate

In the spring of 1984, Mike Carlson and I took a drive into Iowa to see a woman with a huge agate. Maynard Green had told me about the rock and said I should run down and see it. New Haven is barely five miles south of the Minnesota border and is a quaint little farm community. Myrtle Counsell invited us into her home and asked me to pick up the agate. Well into her seventies, she had to have other people move the heavy rock.

When I asked her to tell us how her husband found the rock, she perked up like it happened yesterday. "Ernie didn't find that agate." She said that in 1958, two young boys had found it along a creek that runs through their farm. Ernie was on the tractor plowing when he saw them dragging it across the field. He recognized it as an agate and told the kids to scram. He figured it had come off his property, so it belonged to him. I'm not sure why Myrtle volunteered the story, but it must have been to set the record straight.

It was by far the biggest glacial agate I had seen then, and it still is. The agate is completely banded with areas of thin floating bands in a dense clear chalcedony. There are two big, prominent faces on the stone. One is a finely banded, red and white, comma-shaped pattern that sticks out on the side. The other is a bold, heart-shaped pattern of bright white, floating bands in a sea of smoky quartz. Several areas on the rock have clusters of well developed calcite crystal impressions.

One aspect of this remarkable agate that makes it unique, besides its record-setting size, is its wind-polished surface. In the distant past, the agate must have spent a prolonged period of time out in the open where strong winds could whip over it. Powerful catabatic winds must have poured off a massive glacier punishing everything in its path. The smooth texture was produced by years of sandblasting by a process called ventification. This unique geologic feature provided the finishing touch on a truly special Lake Superior agate treasure.

9. The Bread Loaf

Around 1986 I made my first road trip down to the Lincoln, Nebraska, area to visit a few Lake Superior agate collectors. I stopped at the home of David Meyers in Weeping Water, Nebraska, to see what he had. I looked into his case and was stunned by what I saw. He had several wonderful agates, but one clearly stood out from the rest. I instinctively reached for it and bumped my hand into the glass. Dave laughed and pulled it out for me to look at more closely. It was spectacular. He told me that he bought the agate from a farmer sometime in the late 1960s. It was found in a field near Long Prairie, Minnesota. It took me thirteen years to finally come up with the right Laguna agates to finally trade the stone from Dave.

I traded two fantastic Laguna agates for the "Crown River Agate" and the "Bread Loaf" with Dave Meyers in July of 1999. Judging from those smiles it seems as though both collectors were happy with the deal.

This agate is not shaped like a loaf of bread, nor, unlike the rest of the Top Ten, is it gigantic. At 2.22 pounds, it has every quality that an agate can have to make it great. First, it has a beautiful, cylindrical shape with both ends rounded smooth. Second, each end has a spectacular, large, banded face that makes it seem like two fantastic agates in one. Third, the intense cherry red and bright white banding brings to mind Christmas candy-cane colors. Last, this agate has that rare, beautifully smooth texture from ventification. Whenever people scan my agate collection, they always stop at the Bread Loaf and pick it up. This "one-in-a-million" agate does that to people every single time.

Jim Moore of Balsam Lake, Wisconsin, at the first Night of the Lake Superior Agates in May 1987.

8. The Moore Agate

I first saw this agate at the Night of the Lake Superior Agates in May 1987. It was in the back of a display case and basically went unnoticed by most of the other collectors. I managed to find the owner and asked to take a picture of him with his big agate. Jim Moore said he found the stone in a farm field near Balsam Lake, Wisconsin, in the mid-1940s. After a year and a half of trying unsuccessfully to contact him, I gave the lead to Bob Reineck to see if he could track him down. Bob showed up in my office a couple of weeks later and sold me the prize. At 6.38 pounds the agate is huge, with an elongate, flat shape. It's smooth surface has one glacial break that exposes fine, internal shadow banding. The Moore Agate is one of very few that would be described as white and red rather than the more usual red and white.

7. Jingle Bells

Few agates of any size are found with a perfectly smooth, beach-washed surface. The larger the agate, the more rare this texture is. To have a perfect water-washed stone at 4.21 pounds is virtually unheard of. David Stodola was collecting agates with his family outside Cloquet, Minnesota, in 1977. They were looking in the sandy gravel of a golf course that was under construction. David spotted what looked like a small agate in the sand and began to uncover it. The agate kept getting bigger until the gorgeous trophy appeared. The wide white banding snakes around the surface, producing a spectacular display highlighted with black and red colors. It's one of the few agates that can be rolled across the floor like a bowling ball due to its round shape and exceptionally smooth husk. Dave sold the agate to Jim Haase at the Beaver Bay Agate Shop in 1988 for $1,000. When Jim traded it to me around Christmas that same year, we sat in my kitchen and decided to give it a name. He said that because it was so spectacular, every time he looked at it, it was like "bells going off." I looked at Jim and said, "Why don't we call it Jingle Bells?"

6. The Engagement Agate

The first time I visited George Flaim at his home, the crown jewel of his collection was this 5.75 pounder. George said the agate was found by a Boy Scout on the north beach of Island Lake sometime around 1930. The boy's instructor on the trip ended up with the gem and kept it until his death in 1983. A son-in-law sold it to George at the Moose Lake Agate Days show that same summer. This special stone has many qualities that make it exceptional. It has a perfect nodular shape and fine shadow banding in the large, majestic face. The brown and gray banding contrast beautifully with the hematite-rich red husk. The agate eventually became Janet's engagement gift to me, through some nifty negotiating with George in the summer of 1985. It will always hold sentimental value for our family.

David Stodola holds "Jingle Bells" at the Moose Lake show in 1988. He found the agate in the sandy gravel of a golf course that was under construction near Cloquet, Minnesota in 1977.

5. The Berghuis Agate

Lyle Berghuis was, without a doubt, the toughest person I had ever negotiated with for a Lake Superior Agate. It took five years and countless offers before we finally made a deal. I'll never forget the day he pulled it out of his car in August 1985. I was stunned! A perfect, pill-shaped 6.38-pound stone with rich, dark, earthy colors. The colors include blood red, olive green, lavender and white. To top it off, the shadow banding pattern at the center of the face is in the shape of the letter "P." Even the agate knew it was perfect.

Lyle found the agate in 1972 while picking with his ten-year-old daughter Debbie. On the cold November day I bought it in 1990, he took me to the same gravel pit, a couple of miles north of Milaca. When we returned to the house, Lyle's wife, Betty, told a story about what happened when she and Lyle went on a recent vacation. Their children and grandchildren stayed at their home. Before they left, the family had a talk about what they should do if something happened to them. After they left, the five grandchildren went through the house putting pieces of paper with their names on items they would want. Betty said that when they returned, there were white tags on everything in the house. Only a few items had more than one tag. The big agate that Grandpa found had five tags on it.

As I picked up the agate to head home, Betty began to cry. She said it was like a member of the family was leaving and never coming back. I told her she could

An understandably pleased Lyle Berghuis holding his fantastic find during a 1988 visit.

come see the agate anytime and that it was off to see the world. I'll always do my best to ensure that people can always see and enjoy it.

4. Strawberry Point

Father Graf was a preacher in Festina, Iowa, who acquired many fine agates in the 1950s and 1960s. He happened upon this delightful gem being used as a doorstop in the home of a man who worked at a fish hatchery in Strawberry Point, Iowa. The man reportedly found the agate in a streambed in Backbone State Park near the town. He said the rock looked like a big strawberry, so that's what he called it. Father Graf worked hard for several years trying to get the big agate, and eventually succeeded. Years later, he sold his agate collection to a friend, who in turn sold it to Gene Burry, a Methodist minister from Greene, Iowa. In 1988, he traded the big agate to Bob Reineck, who traded it to me a few days later. The agate is mind-blowing in both size (7.41 pounds) and quality. The huge fortification face with "fleshy" color on the top side puts it in the top ten.

3. The Six-Pound Red-and-White

The six-pound red-and-white received several votes as the number one agate in the poll. There's no question it's the boldest and brightest laker of all time. At 6.16 pounds, it has monstrous size with massive red and white bands approaching three-fourths of an inch thick. An agate is said to be a showstopper if you can see the pattern from across the room. The pattern in this agate is so spectacular it can be seen from a city block away.

The agate was found in a farm field near Randall, Minnesota, sometime around 1980. Harold Schmidt bought the agate from the discoverer for $100. Harold sold it to Maynard Green for $300. It was in Maynard's display case when I first saw the agate. He had many beautiful specimens, but this one made the others look sick. In 1986, Mike Smith and Jim Null from the Lincoln, Nebraska, area purchased Maynard's Lake Superior agate collection and split it up between them. Mike told me that both he and Jim wanted the six-pounder, so they decided to flip a coin. The winner had the first pick (the six-pound red-and-white), and the loser received the next two picks. Mike smiled from ear to ear as he told me how he won the toss. Both Mike and Jim were active in the hobby and made trips up into Minnesota with their agates. The six-pounder was a big hit at the first Night of the

Lake Superior Agates. A couple of years later, Mike called and told me he was thinking of selling the big one. I flew down to see him and to attend the 1990 Lincoln Gem and Mineral Show. I must have caught Mike at a weak moment because he eventually put a price on the six-pounder. Even though it was a big price, I didn't hesitate a second. The opportunity to acquire a once-in-a-lifetime agate like this doesn't come along very often. It was an easy decision.

The six-pound red-and-white was one of nine of Maynard Green's best agates I picked out during a 1984 visit.

2. The Ham Agate

When I first pulled this giant from the grocery bag Harold Johnston had put in front of me, I almost fell over. It was the spring of 1985, and he had acquired the agate in a trade for $1,000 worth of kitchen cabinetwork. The woman who gave up the rock was the daughter of the discoverer, Nina Cox. Nina found the agate sometime before 1921 while walking in a field with her husband Robert. She believed until her death at age 93 that what she had found was a petrified ham. I have personally seen only a dozen Lake Superior agates over ten pounds. This 10.25-pounder is by far the best. The reddish-orange, glassy husk encloses well-developed, multicolored banding that pours out the top into a bull's eye pattern. The agate resembles a candy-colored, one-billion year-old tree stump. It is this giant gemstone that often recurs in my big agate fantasies.

1. The Minnehaha Falls Agate

The Lake Superior agate voted the number one specimen of all time is not the biggest, brightest, or boldest. However, it has a good share of all these qualities. The one aspect of this agate that impressed people the most is its history with Native Americans. All the other top agates have a relatively short history with humans, the longest less than ninety years. The history of the Minnehaha Falls Agate goes back at least hundreds, and perhaps thousands of years.

I first wrote about this agate shortly after I acquired it (The Lake Superior Agate, 3rd ed. [Edina: Burgess Publishing, 1996]). I have since learned a little more. At the end of the evening for the Night of the Lake Superior Agates II, a man approached me as I was packing up my collection. He was a relatively short, thin man with long graying dark hair. He introduced himself and said he was of Native American descent. He asked if he could look at the Falls Agate I had talked about during my slide presentation. He sat down on the floor and began to study the agate very intently. I watched him out of the corner of my eye as he carefully studied the stone and gently felt the groove with his fingers. After a few moments he put it down in front of him, sat back, and said, "It's authentic, alright." I was puzzled and said, "What?" He looked up at me and said, "It's a skull crusher." I couldn't believe my ears.

He explained what he meant. The pecking groove was very carefully made to secure the agate to the top end of a small sapling that was then used as a staff. The agate staff was used for special ceremonies to smash the skulls of animals, releasing their spirits. These freed spirits would ensure good hunting, weather, and health. He said that this agate would have been very sacred to the tribe and was probably passed on for generations, perhaps a thousand years or more.

I was dumbfounded as I listened to him. After all the speculation about this agate, this explanation made the most sense. It was too big to be used as a weapon or everyday tool. It also seemed reasonable that Native Americans would have greatly appreciated such a rare and beautiful stone. They probably cherished it as much, or more than, modern-day rock hounds.

We will never know for sure what the actual history of this remarkable agate is. All we can do is wonder, who was the lucky person who first found it, and how did it end up along the muddy creek bank at the foot of Minnehaha Falls? Wouldn't it be fascinating to know the journey it has taken?

To commemorate this magnificent gemstone I commissioned Dan Wiemer to do a painting that captures important moments in the stone's history (see page 43).

Onward
We Go

As we move into the new millennium, the future of the Lake Superior agate hobby looks brighter than ever. Even though we've lost a few of the older collectors, many new, energetic people are jumping into the fray. Overall, it seems like people everywhere are realizing a new appreciation for natural things. Fossils, minerals, and other natural resources are not just passing fads being taken for granted. It seems that people are finally showing the respect for finite resources that they deserve.

There's also hope on the horizon for agate pickers. The biggest challenge is obtaining permission to pick in the best places to find the elusive laker, gravel pits. As quality gravel resources become less plentiful, the price for aggregate will steadily increase. Many current aggregate producers are finding it more difficult to purchase property with good material and to obtain permits to operate on the land they do have. From a public relations standpoint, it would help to use a resource that aggregate producers currently take for granted. They could implement a program so that agate enthusiasts could collect at certain times and places. Not only would this help public opinion and make obtaining permits easier, but far fewer agates would end up in concrete and asphalt. To ease liability concerns, anyone who wanted to collect agates would have to obtain a state rock-hounding license. Collectors could take classes about safety, and quarry operators could groom the pits to lessen potential danger. An arrangement like this could benefit everybody, especially our precious state gemstone.

As for me personally, I figure if I'm lucky the second half of my life just kicked off. I have a wonderful wife and family that give me inspiration and support every day, especially in the manic hobby I pursue. I think about my dad everyday. But I don't get as sad as I used to. In fact, whenever I think about him, a big smile comes to my face. In the twenty-two years I knew him, we did more fun things together than most fathers and sons do in a lifetime. I do feel bad, sometimes, that Grant and Amanda were never able to meet him. But as long as Janet and I are around, they will always know about him.

My agate addiction is well into the full-blown stage, and I realized long ago that there is no cure. Hopefully, the years ahead will be filled with many more Lake Superior agate adventures. You can be sure that I will do everything I can to try and make things happen.

People Of Agate

In this section I wanted to picture some of the people I've known during my agate travels. As I was looking at these photos with a friend, he said it seemed all the rock hounds I knew in the early days were older folks. He was right. In the early 1980s when I started chasing after agates, most of the people collecting them were older. It was a testament to the status of the hobby at that time. You'll notice that as we move closer to 2000, a younger crowd has entered the hobby. A changing of the guard is definitely taking place. I just happened to be one of the first to come along in the present generation of rock-hounds. I'll always cherish the memories of the time I spent with the collectors who are no longer with us, and look forward to more fun with the collectors I know now, as well as the ones to come. I hope they look back someday and say they had a good time with me.

In Memory
Bill Boltz (see page 81)
Bill Funk
John Kammerer (see page 71)
Ken Johnson
Harold Johnston (see page 31)
Albert Peterson (see page 77)
Leo "Rocky" Quinn
Ted Vanasse

Pickers
Charlie Clark
Greg and Hope Clark
Jim Haase
Craig Litchey
Pat Malmsten
Carrie Ohme
Jennifer Pitoscia
Jim Rodeski
Cory Schulte
Dan Wiemer
Terri Whipple

Collectors
Group Shot
Maynard Green
John Harris
Jesse Shepherd, Grant and Amanda Wolter
Mike Smith

Bill and Shirley Funk at the 1992 Moose Lake Agate Days show.

Ken Johnson and I during a January 1984 visit.

Leo "Rocky" Quinn shows Bruce Grant a large petrified log at his Beaver Bay Agate Shop in 1983.

Ted Vanasse of Spring Valley, Wisconsin, shared many rare specimens he collected, including this mammoth tusk, during a 1985 visit. Mr. Vanasse wrote the first book about Lake Superior agates in 1949.

Charlie Clark in February 2001 with three big ones he found in 1999. Hard to believe, but even a die-hard Green Bay Packer fan can find good agates.

Greg and Hope Clark with their gem in February 1999.

Jim Haase at my house the day he traded Jingle Bells to me in 1988. I gave up four nice agates over two pounds to get it.

Craig Litchey of Fish Lake, Minnesota, shows off two beautiful lakers he found at the 1998 Moose Lake show.

Pat Malmsten (Size Twelve) in February 2001 holds two beauties he found during our late 1980s agate wars.

Carrie Ohme at the 2000 Moose Lake Show with the great stone she found two months earlier.

George Flaim's daughter Jennifer Pitoscia shows off two of her prize large lakers at the 1999 Moose Lake show.

Jim Rodeski with a one pound beauty in May of 1999.

Cory Schulte with his trophy agate in November 1996.

Dan Wiemer is not only a terrific artist, he's also a pretty good agate picker. In this February 2001 photo he shows off two supers he found in 1999.

Terri Whipple with her three-pound beauty in December 2000.

168

Several of the die-hard collectors gather in my basement for an agate powwow in November 2000. Left to right: Bill Steffes, Charlie White, John Marshall, Mike Carlson, Mike Pendzimas, Bruce Strohschein, myself, David Meyers, and Bruce Peddle.

Maynard Green and I at the 1999 Moose Lake Show.

John Harris holds a recent four-pound acquisition in December 2000.

Instead of lemonade, Jesse Shepherd along with Grant and Amanda sell Pokemon cards and Lake Superior agates on the street corner in June of 2000.

Mike Smith in May 1987 with his showstopping six-pound, red and white agate.

Acknowledgments

All photos in this book were taken by the author except for the following:

Page	Photographer
2	Bruce Peddle
4	Glory Days Photography (Tim Gabrielson)
11	Minneapolis Star-Tribune
13	Unknown
17	Janet Wolter
19	Mark Brugman
24	United States Air Force
25	United States Military Police
48	Aloha Photography
59	Richard Olsenius
65	Bruce Peddle
72	John Marshall
88	Unknown
91	Minnesota State Capitol Photographer
92	Janet Wolter
100	Janet Wolter
137	Jake Anderson
140	Jake Anderson
146	Terri Whipple
164	#2 Unknown
167	#11 Bruce Peddle
169	#15 Diana Watters
169	#16 Steve Nyquist
Back Cover	Joe Rossi/St. Paul Pioneer Press

Epilogue

As this book goes to print, it occurred to me to mention an emerging aspect of Lake Superior agate collecting that already has had great impact - the internet. It is now bringing our magnificent gemstone to a worldwide audience. I recently made my first purchase on ebay of a large and terrific specimen. The seller was somebody I might never have otherwise known about. The power of the internet is unlimited and I have decided to give it a try by launching my own website (www.lakesuperior-agate.com). My hope is to enhance the overall Lake Superior agate experience for all those who visit the site.

I was able to outbid another buyer by $1.50 for this terrific specimen on ebay. The Conrad Agate was found in a gravel pit one mile west of Moose Lake, Minnesota, by an unknown teenage boy in 1958. Gordon Conrad was picking agates in the pit when the boy introduced himself and eventually sold the agate he had recently found.

Order Form

(tear along perforation)

To commemorate the new book, The Lake Superior Agate - One Man's Journey, Scott F. Wolter commissioned two watercolor paintings. Lake Superior Agate, Inc. is offering a low run number of 500 limited edition prints, each signed by both the artist and author. Also for purchase, is Scott's previous book, "The Lake Superior Agate, 3/e."

"One In A Million" (see front cover) - This beautiful Lake Superior North Shore scene captures a quiet family moment before their patient pursuit is pleasantly rewarded.
Print Size: 26 1/2" x 21 3/4" • Price: $125

"The Minnehaha Falls Agate" (see page 43) - Important moments in the rich history of this unique Lake Superior agate including it's modern discovery at historic Minnehaha Falls in Minneapolis, Minnesota.
Print Size: 29" x 21" • Price: $125

"The Lake Superior Agate - Third Edition" by Scott F. Wolter - This book has 125 pages of valuable information which includes:
- 62 color photographs of prized Lake Superior agates
- Description of Lake Superior agates types and their formation
- Personal stories of encounters with agate collectors
- Where to go and what to look for when collecting Lake Superior agates
- Glossary of geological terms
- Over 15,000 copies sold since the first edition was published in November of 1986
Paperback Format 8 1/2" x 11" • Price: $30.95

Name _____

Address _____

City _____ MN_____ Zip Code _____

Email _____ Phone _____

I would like to order:

	Quantity	Price	Shipping	Total
"One In A Million"	_____	$125	$5	_____
"The Minnehaha Falls Agate"	_____	$125	$5	_____
"The Lake Superior Agate - Third Edition"	_____	$30.95	$4	_____
"The Lake Superior Agate-One Man's Journey"	_____	$42.95	$4	_____
			Grand Total*	_____

*Minnesota residents please add 6.5% sales tax.

Please enclose a check for the above amount with this order form and mail to:
Lake Superior Agate, Inc. • P.O. Box 14611 • Minneapolis, MN 55414.